T

C000182569

The Thirteen Signs of the Zodiac

Walter Berg

Thorsons
An Imprint of HarperCollins*Publishers*

Thorsons
An Imprint of HarperCollins*Publishers*
77–85 Fulham Palace Road
Hammersmith, London W6 8JB
1160 Battery Street
San Francisco, California 94111–1213

Published by Thorsons 1995
10 9 8 7 6 5 4 3 2 1

A catalogue record for this book
is available from the British Library

ISBN 0 7225 3254 7

Printed in Great Britain by
HarperCollinsManufacturing Glasgow

Contents

Introduction

The Thirteen Signs of the Zodiac will influence the way
you see yourself in an essential and positive way.
Understanding your new (and true) Sun Sign will
enable you to see for the first time the real you, your
genuine personality.

In this fast-changing and uncertain world it is
important to know yourself, who you really are. This
knowledge will enrich and elevate you and give you
a newfound self-confidence.

Because most modern astrologers have used the
traditional Star Signs of the Zodiac (not the actual
Star Signs under which people were born), they have
presented you with a false portrait of yourself. This is
unfortunate because when you are making important
choices in life – choices about your relationships,
career, health and finance – it is crucial that you
receive sound advice. You now have the opportunity
to make informed decisions about your life, based on
your New Star Sign.

Many of the perceptions you have had about yourself, therefore, have not been accurate. The views
you hold about your personality have, even though
you may not think so, been influenced by modern
astrology. When you have read your Star Sign details
in the newspaper or elsewhere, have you ever said
to yourself: 'What a load of rubbish, this is nothing
like me!'? In spite of this gut reaction, your modern

astrological profile has subtly affected the way you visualize yourself. All those little irksome mannerisms attributed to you which you felt (deep inside) were not true? Well, you were right – they weren't you! Put all those bothersome details behind you. This book will show you in your true light. The New You will amaze and delight you. 'Yes, this is really me. This is just how I feel,' you will find yourself saying. It is time you heard the truth about yourself.

'The Sun does not move,' wrote Leonardo da Vinci in 1495. Well, everything in the Cosmos moves, including the Sun, the Earth and the Star Signs of the Zodiac. The Signs of the Zodiac were first mapped by the ancient Babylonians about 3,000 years ago when, indeed, there were 12 Star Signs. Movement on the Cosmic time-scale is very slow compared with the time-scale of a human life. The Star Signs are slipping by a small amount each year, so that there are now 13 Signs in the Zodiac. The Sign of Ophiuchus (30 November–17 December) moved into the Zodiac over 1,000 years ago. Most astrologers continued to use the traditional 12 Signs of the Zodiac because they were unaware of star movements. That practice has continued to the present day. To illustrate just how slowly the Cosmic clock advances: the Age of Pisces replaced the Age of Aries about 1,400 years ago, and the much-heralded Age of Aquarius will not be here for another 600 years!

The New Pisces

First Sign of the Zodiac:
12 March to 18 April

- Ruling planets: *Neptune and Jupiter*
- Element: *Water*
- Quality: *Mutable*
- Best Signs for Love: *Aries, Leo (Libra, Aquarius)*

Personality

The vast expanse and hidden depths of the boundless oceans represent the fluid and changing nature of the New Piscean. You are emotionally very sensitive and can even sense the feelings of others. Some have called this gift you have 'empathic'; it is so strong that you are said to possess a sixth sense. Let us be honest, New Piscean, you bear little resemblance to your traditional Star Sign profile: selfish, aggressive and quick-tempered. How could anyone have said such things about someone as sensitive and receptive to others' needs as you are? The New Pisces replaces one Star Sign (Aries) as well as keeping almost one third of 'old Pisces'.

1

Jupiter, one of your ruling planets, represents the life principles of expansion and growth, complementing your New Piscean sensitivity. Neptune (your other ruler) is the god of the ocean and of the underworld waterways, and influences you in the most subtle ways through a process of refining and reflecting, giving you clarity of vision.

The New Pisces is now the first Star Sign of the Zodiac and not the twelfth. This is important to you. Being first and not last enhances your self-confidence and self-esteem. Come on, New Piscean, you have much self-worth and can now go for it in a big way. You are adaptable and able to enjoy variety. Enjoying variety does not make you restless or fickle, as your traditional Star Sign may have indicated. No way! Being involved in many different activities and projects, enjoying a wide range of cultural and sporting interests, (as you always have done but were afraid to admit to), makes you a very interesting person.

Your easy-going nature attracts others to you. Friends who need a shoulder to cry on will inevitably come to you. You have a kindness, sympathy and depth of compassion not matched by any other Star Sign. You possess an inner strength but you can, if you are caught off-guard, be moved to tears. It is said that you cannot bear the suffering of others. Through your empathic powers you do actually feel and share the suffering of those in anguish, whether physical or emotional. You are more than a witness, and this is why you recoil as you register others' despair.

Your empathic power leads you into the world of the psychic. Yes, your interest in the mystical and psychical can now be explained in the light of your New Star Sign, and this may come as a shock to you.

2

All those leanings you have felt towards transcendentalism and mysticism, and your interest in astrology (which has been there all the time) are understandable. You no longer need to feel uncomfortable about it! Be yourself! Go with your mystical feeling and explore worlds that others can only dream of, or have no conception of at all.

The two fishes of Pisces are joined together and are pulling in opposite directions – typical of the dual nature of the New Piscean. There are numerous references in the New Testament to fishes and the positive teachings of all antiquity – love, self-reunification and service to others – are embodied in them. You are, indeed, a combination of paradoxes and opposites. You are fishing among lots of alternatives and searching for vision and a mystical connection.

Your enigmatic behaviour may appear bizarre to others, but to you everything is relative. Your double-edged approach often allows you to see both sides of an argument, and this ability breeds tolerance. It is good that fanaticism is alien to you – if only more of the ruthless characters from history had been New Pisceans, wars, territorial claims and bigotry could not have occurred. This wide viewpoint does not judge. You appear to be indifferent. You fail to take a stance even when abuse is thrown at you. Issues that are important to others can never be taken too seriously by you, because you have knowledge, through your gift of empathy, of all aspects of an issue. You appreciate the beauty of the whole crystal in your hand, where others see just one surface at a time. Your lack of worldliness is compensated for by your inner life and imagination. You have no limits. Many great creative scientists, composers and artists were

New Pisceans. Your imagination, like the ocean, seems boundless. You hold the secret of life and the key to the unconscious; this is why you sometimes have a problem coping with reality. You tend to overlook simple things: not paying a utility bill, leaving the oven switched on until the meal burns, letting the car insurance expire, etc. The idea of being limited, trapped in a human body, is irritating to the New Piscean.

Your instinctive nature makes you take decisions spontaneously rather than taking a careful approach and planning your actions. However, you are a safe, solid person whom others rely on. You will always be there for others, and your boundless world of dreams rather than reality will endear you to others.

Some time ago I was at a loose end. A New Piscean friend of mine suggested, on the spur of the moment, that we head out into the country for the afternoon. 'Sounds good to me,' I said. We took my car and left around noon. About 30 miles outside of the city we passed an empty car parked by the roadside. My New Piscean friend asked me to stop. I pulled over. 'What's the matter?' I asked. But I could see the expression on her face, looking into the distance, almost trance-like, and I knew something was wrong. 'I have a feeling,' she replied. We both walked towards the parked car and I was shocked to see the driver slumped over the passenger seat, unconscious! He had fallen from view. I rushed back to my car and phoned for an ambulance while my friend administered first aid. The driver had suffered a heart attack! He is fine now, but had my New Piscean friend not been with me, he may not have survived. This is what I am talking about when I say you are instinctive and that other people, even strangers, can rely on you.

Liza Minelli is a New Piscean. One only has to look at her dark, deep pools of eyes to know that this woman really feels for others. What makes Liza so attractive (besides her talent) is her open-armed warmth towards almost everyone she meets. She genuinely loves everyone. True, she can genuinely dislike people, too, but that never lasts long. She is far too generous-hearted for revenge or spite; and she would feel very uncomfortable if she ever thought that her behaviour had caused someone (anyone!) pain.

William Shatner, also a New Piscean, is a natural diplomat who sees all sides of any argument (yes, as himself, not just as Captain Kirk, up there in space). William has tremendous compassion for others. He can take many knocks in life without reacting violently. He prefers to ask 'Why?' before blaming or condemning anyone. He has an adventurous spirit and his mind, even more than his body, loves 'to boldly go...' (no, I'm not going to say it!)

Love and Relationships

You may become disillusioned with stable relationships or with getting caught up in the cold realities of family life. You are not domesticated, even though you do like your creature comforts. You say you are in love, but do you mean it? Yes, of course you do, but you are always in love – with a new cause, a new fad or a new fashion. You are in love with everything and this can drive your partner crazy. Your lover, who expected a 'normal' relationship, does not know what to make of you. Try to be more responsive if you can. But do not make the mistake of being too submissive. If you are too compliant this may be mistaken for a lack of passion, as if you don't care strongly, even though you do.

Let me tell you of one major flaw that you must watch out for: the ease with which you enter into a relationship. Even on a casual basis you are intensely emotional. This over-zealous approach may send out the wrong signals. You are listening intently to someone of the opposite sex and he or she is flattered that you appear to be paying so much attention. Some will shy away from you, thinking you are coming on too strong, but those who respond to your signals will take advantage. Come on, admit it, New Piscean, you are easily seduced.

As a lover you are interested in everybody and will only become seriously involved with someone after you have 'played the field'. If you say 'I love you' you will mean it; equally, if you later say to the same person 'You meant nothing to me', you will also mean it. It is those little fishes joining together and pulling in reverse directions. Your emotions are always swinging to and fro, leaving no trace of the previous emotion. If your partner is the type who can be possessive and wants you to swear that you will be faithful, then technically you will be faithful, but your imagination may not be so. When you wish to make a lasting commitment you do so with the utmost sincerity and honour. Lamentably, a part of you remains outside the commitment and will always be away across the ocean of imagination.

You are a multi-faceted individual and often cannot decide who you are. You may have several different personalities, beliefs or opinions in one week. When you take on board the persona of all these facets you are playing a kind of mental gymnastics. This leads to confusion for your lover and, without being aware of it, you hurt those you love or with whom you are involved in a deep relationship. You are not deliberately cruel, but your expressions of love are up and down. They are not consistent or straightforward. The New Piscean's loves and relationships will be akin to strange voyages, journeys into the unknown, into worlds full of mystery and mayhem.

I had a client who came to see me last summer. She was feeling down and quite distressed. She told me that she wanted to make a commitment to her partner because she felt that he (a New Libran) was the right one for her. Yes, she loved him, they got on really well together and they had a good sexual relationship. What was the problem? My client's partner did not want to make a permanent commitment to their relationship and my client couldn't understand why. Since she had expressed her wishes to him, his attitude towards her had changed. He continually pointed out small failings in her – the way she dressed, her hairstyle and her little irritating habits. The New Libran was feeling uncertain. My client had disturbed the balance in their relationship by asking for a commitment and the New Libran was feeling vulnerable. There was nothing wrong with his reaction, but my client, because of her (New Piscean) empathic gift and her high emotional state, was picking up so much energy from her partner that it was literally short-circuiting her psyche. I suggested that a short course of meditation would help by switching off her receptiveness to his feelings, which generated tension in her and was adversely affecting their relationship. A couple of weeks later she told me that her partner had agreed to make a commitment to their relationship and that they were planning to get married.

When in a state of high tension you must learn to switch off. Your urge to transcend the material world can sometimes, though not very often, work against you and make you bewildered.

New Pisceans make life for their lovers very romantic. Your nature is romantic and the trappings of intimacy are everywhere in your life and your lover's life. You want to make a fuss of your partner, and most times this is really appreciated even if the response is not always what you expect. You know how to make your partner feel wanted, and your loving and caring nature would make you an ideal partner for any suitable Star Sign.

Your ideal lover would be a New Aries or a New Leo, or perhaps a New Libran or a New Aquarian. Don't look so shocked! These Signs may not be what you expected but they are the Signs for you. New Leo, a Fire element with an exciting roar, ruler of the beasts, would be slightly better for you than the New Aquarian, spouting hot air.

Career

If I were walking up the beach, away from the sea, and I was knocked over by someone rushing to the ocean, that someone would be a New Piscean. You long for the sea, the world of imagination and dreams. Your ideal vocation would be in that direction – not necessarily a sailor, today there are many opportunities on ocean-going cruise liners. These huge ships take on all types of personnel, and this is where you would fit. Your empathic qualities would also make you a good social worker or counsellor. Any type of vocation where will-power and rational thought are *not* essential factors would suit you. A job in which intuitive, sympathetic, imaginative and creative qualities can be exercised and developed is the one for you. A career as a mechanic or a dentist? No way! You are a 'people person', and your career should reflect this.

If you venture out and try for the big time, you may be wonderfully successful or a complete failure – again, the twin but opposing nature of the fishes. You are a natural musician, artist, writer, poet, psychic and spinner of dreams. If you are lucky and 'make it' in one of these fields, then yes, you will be financially secure. The alternative is to end up in honky tonk bars singing to alcohol-dazed audiences and low life. Be careful here. You can keep down a 'regular' job, you know, and still live within the world of the imagination. 'Moderation is a virtue only in those who are thought to have an alternative,' Henry Kissinger once said. You have got alternatives, so moderation is truly a virtue that you will have to strive for, throughout your life. If you at least aim for moderation, then you'll stand a chance of some order in your life. But you'll never be bored or boring, that's for sure. You will always land on your feet financially. That is how it is. Knowing about your financial security is good, but don't think you can now rush out on a spending spree!

Health

Poor old feet! Yes, you know, don't you? Your tendency to feet problems lies in a reflex association with your abdomen. Be kind to your feet and look after them. When they feel tired and aching, fill a bowl full of hot water and pour in salts and fragrances. Let your feet have a good soak. Ooh! Ah! Just what the doctor ordered. You are a cold-blooded creature (fish), and though you mentally hanker after what is across the ocean, your feet do not like to be too cold or wet (another anomaly brought on by the dual polarity of the fish). You are in harmony within yourself and manage to link body and spirit together, which provides you with inner strength. This is lucky because without it you might be prone to mild nervous or emotional tension.

Do not develop a weakness for alcohol, and if you need to take drugs for any condition, don't go overboard with them! It is worth mentioning that many alternative remedies would suit you. Next time you have the chance, visit an alternative health centre and have a chat with the people there about your health generally. See what advice they offer. There is no harm in trying their tonics, and if they listen to you properly they can be a great help.

Future

The ocean beckons, firing your imagination. Your future is limited only by the limitations of your imagination. New Piscean, you have the rare gift to empathize with others. You have an uncanny ability to share another person's emotions, which other Star Signs do not possess. Yes, the ocean calls, but keep your feet firmly on dry land (apart from the odd cruise) and your future will be secure. You are receptive, very impressionable, intuitive and subtle, with a strong creative imagination. Though you are emotionally sensitive, Jupiter (Zeus) is with you and Neptune working with Jupiter will see you through.

New Piscean, you are a wonderful person and you and your partner are destined to have a satisfying and loving relationship which will bring much happiness to both of you and which will be a stabilizing influence on you. Your world will continue to expand and grow; your experience – both psychically and in the material world – will grow, too. Personal development and growth are important to you and will aid your future life with friends, family and love.

The New Aries

Second Sign of the Zodiac:
19 April to 13 May

- Ruling planet: *Mars*
- Element: *Fire*
- Quality: *Cardinal*
- Best Signs for Love: *Pisces, Scorpio, Ophiuchus (Taurus, Virgo)*

Personality

'I want the best and I want it yesterday' could well be the slogan of the New Aries. You're an impatient and self-assertive Sign and will travel far through enterprise and sheer will-power. Those born on 19 or 20 April were and still are Aries. You are now joined by those born after 20 April (formerly Taureans).

The New Aries is not stubborn, nor do you slavishly adhere to rules. Good lord, no! Your old Sign qualities were quite mistakenly attributed to you. Your (true) go-getting attitude is not, however, really about self-advancement (though it often achieves that result), you can also be a champion for the underdog. You like to promote worthy causes. Championing others can heighten your reputation in the hierarchy of politics, business and in society generally. Yet you are not a self-seeking person. After all, you are quite blunt and to the point, often upsetting others by your forthright and, I must say, often rude remarks. You won't cowtow to anyone to safeguard your position. George Bernard Shaw once said: 'The secret of success is to offend the greatest number of people,' but go easy, please!

It is worth noting that your ruling planet is Mars, the god of war, and you are a true warrior with a pioneering and adventurous spirit. You like to take chances and many will see you as foolhardy rather than courageous. Your previous ruling planet was Venus, whose energy was supposed to make you unfocused. How untrue! You are a Positive and a Cardinal Sign: self-expressive and enterprising. The New Aries is larger than life, go-ahead and capable of achieving results fast.

In common with all Fire Signs, New Aries is also a child in spirit and this, of course, means that you can behave like a child, either in the most mean-spirited way or in the most 'innocently generous' way. When you have plans (perhaps a business plan) you can get heated up and become wild over the various facets to your plan. You throw yourself into the project and your energy and enthusiasm appear unlimited. Often others get tired just watching you run around, chasing one project after another.

You seem naturally courageous and fearless and have a will of iron. You may often be unaware of the fact that others might wish to put forward a different idea from your own. You perceive this as a conflict and are unable to look objectively at it. Your horizons become closed and you are genuinely hurt when others challenge you and call you selfish. Aries is the Ram, and the horns of a ram are symbolic of your character: thrusting, aggressive, leader of the flock, always ready to accept a challenge. Life with the New Aries may be difficult. If those around you do not like action, high energy and a hectic life, they may assume that you are totally selfish and, perhaps, hyperactive. You may be quiet for a period, but you will, without warning, jump to your feet and charge off to the next project with as much energy as if this were your first and most exciting enterprise. It is the spirit of competition, the urge to win in any situation that drives the New Aries on. Not only do New Aries have this power in business but also in the mental realm, as scholars. You love a challenge and you love to win. One problem for you to watch is that when you fail to see the other point of view you can easily become disillusioned and bitter. Others may not share your values, yet this you refuse to recognize.

Your generous nature can land you in trouble, because you mostly trust people. You believe the best about them. When others have it in for you and begin stabbing you in the back, you are genuinely bewildered by their actions. You are not devious. You have no time for underhand plots and petty vendettas. You would do well to remember, however, that some people are like that.

An acquaintance of mine came to see me last autumn. She was feeling down and slightly paranoid. She informed me that her business partners were conspiring against her to ruin a promotion deal she was setting up. Some way into our conversation it became apparent that she had not consulted her colleagues first about the promotion and had, in effect, forced her plans through. When other team members raised objections she took it personally and assumed they were attempting to disrupt her campaign. I said to her: 'You are a New Aries. Try consulting with other team members and use a little applied psychology on them. Say how much you value their opinions and input.' This she did, after which her promotional campaign and her working relationships were much more successful. If you do not compromise with life or people, this attitude may not serve you well. In a bygone age when societies were more tribal, you could go out and conquer and spread your message. Today we live in complex societies and a balance, a happy medium, must be the goal.

André Agassi is a New Aries – strong, energetic and charismatic. How can anyone fail to follow his lead and revere him as a true star? Not as controversial a figure as John McEnroe, André nevertheless does not shy away from saying exactly what is on his mind or from doing what he knows is right for him. He has this golden self-confidence and self-assurance that also gives him a very attractive, glowing aura.

Bianca Jagger, a New Aries with a burning cause in her heart at all times, leaps into action whenever she feels her talents can be harnessed to do good. She, like Agassi, has tremendous sex appeal. Life for Bianca, as for all New Aries, must offer challenges for her to conquer. Once conquered, she is ready for the next hurdle.

15

Love and Relationships

Fiery Mars reaches every part of your psyche. You are not particularly tactful in relationships, especially if you have been with a partner for a long period of time. If your partner (or any of your friends) is passive, you will tend to dominate – yet you find this frustrating because then there is no challenge. Inevitably, one-sided arguments with your partner will be a common feature in such a relationship. You will be shadow-boxing with yourself and will find it very unstimulating. You see, New Aries, you love the battle, you love the pursuit. You see someone you feel may be interesting to you and you must find out, you must know. It is the chase, the adventure, that drives your passions. Once you feel you have conquered your prey, the excitement is over. You and your conquered partner sit quietly together and there is no real passion. Your imagination drifts off elsewhere into another dimension and on to the next chase, the next cause. Life is all one big game to you and (to paraphrase Shakespeare) 'there is the rub. For in that sleep of tedium, what dreams may come?'

What happens after you get together with someone you like or love? When you were securing your prey, you embarked upon an endless strategy of love letters, gifts, surprises and other extreme tokens of affection to win the prize you were seeking. Once the chase is over, you become almost a phantom figure and are bored with the tedium and endless 'sameness' of a stable relationship. You are obsessed with what you cannot have rather than with what you have got – your true love. However, despair not! You can, in spite of your mental roving, be very loyal and faithful to your partner and to your friends. It's just that you become a little restless in a situation that never changes or, more to the point, does not provide enough challenges to meet your needs. There is nothing more exciting and stimulating to the New Aries than a difficulty or a conflict which you can resolve. You will stick with your partner once you have made the commitment – especially if your partner is strong and someone you cannot dominate – but your relationship will always be linked with your love of challenge. You may experience several 'practice runs' before you settle with the right person.

Some time ago, a client came to see me about a personal crisis she was encountering. Her relationship with her lover was in the doldrums and she didn't know why. She and her lover had been together for just over a year. At the beginning of the relationship everything was fine – in fact it had been the happiest and most exciting time of her life. 'What has gone wrong?' she sighed. 'I really thought this relationship was it.' Because I have always worked with the true Star Signs, my client was already aware that she was a New Aries. However, she had not really thought too much about the implications of her Star Sign for her current personal relationship. The problems she and her lover were experiencing arose not because they were wrong for each other, but because she had not made an effort to vary their relationship. Had she looked more carefully at her New Star Sign profile, she would have recognized her predicament. 'Change your hairstyle or your wardrobe, try a different restaurant with new faces, move house, take a holiday,' I advised. My client needed change. New Aries people need change; without it they wither and die. My client was receptive to my counselling and she is again experiencing a good and rewarding relationship with her lover. We may not be able to change the universe but we can, with a little knowledge of our Star Signs, change our personal circumstances and make life work for us rather than letting life bore us to death.

Your extraordinary quality – and the one quality that makes you such an exciting and fascinating person to be with – is your love of change. Change is everything to you: a new house, a new job, a new task, even a change in yourself is what keeps you happy. If you are in a relationship which does not develop and grow, you can effectively change such an association by making it your new goal or cause. You are very passionate, with strong sexual feelings, but you are not particularly refined or tactful; in your sexual play, you will lean towards the adventurous.

Your ideal lover would be a New Piscean, a New Scorpio or a New Ophiuchan. New Taureans and New Virgoans are possibilities. You have a lot of Signs to choose from; any one of these would be good for you. New Scorpio: a Water element to drown your passion; New Ophiuchus: another Water Sign but with Mutable qualities to tolerate your changeableness and to complement your enterprising nature.

Career

Organizations which are looking for a leader to pull through a new mission statement or a change in corporate policy need look no further. The New Aries is a leader, one who effects change and inspires others to change. In a situation where a company needs to change in order to remain competitive, no one can manage change better than a New Aries. Your pioneering spirit can be harnessed and used to instigate change. You love change, thrive on it and actively encourage it. Your 'old' star Sign job profile: 'one who should not take chances, or risk a sudden change; where perseverance and routine are advised' was so wrong for you. This is why, if you did listen to that advice, given sincerely, you may have been led into erroneous career choices. The boring civil servant who takes a tea break at 10 a.m., punctually, every day, and leaves the office at 5 p.m. prompt – that's never you, is it? Take this advice: go for a career that will use and value your natural talent of leadership. Not only will you thrive in large organizations but you can make a contribution in many situations.

You are not a steady, introverted plodder, nor are you one of life's slaves to rules and regulations. You are quick-witted, quick-thinking and like to initiate action. Perhaps the City or Wall Street, where the stakes are high and are changing minute by minute, would suit you best? You are not the reflective type and academia would not thrill you. A philosopher poring over ancient, musty manuscripts? No way! You are a starter and a finisher. You see a job through to the end, though you do tend to overlook the details and any possible snags along the way. If you are a member of a team, the success of that team will only work if the other team members are strong. If they are not, you will walk all over them, and your lack of attention to detail may cause confusion.

Financially, you should have little to worry about

if you follow your gut reaction and are mindful of others' reactions and input. Yes, a large financial institution or any other fast-moving money market would suit you. If you do move into industry or the retail or service sector, you will need to be in a fast and changing role. A position of that nature will secure you money and provide you with a rewarding career.

Health

Your fast-moving, fast-thinking and forever-changing lifestyle is not without its health problems. Your proneness to severe headaches, migraine and eye strain are all linked with the vitality of your life. Stress can cause backache and neuralgia. Take my advice: pamper yourself every week. Book yourself in for the full treatment – a full massage – come on, you can afford it and you can afford to take the time off from other activities. (Yes, you *can*.) You will find that a full body massage, especially around the shoulder area and lower back, most beneficial. Lie on the massage table and relax for about an hour. Let yourself completely unwind, and leave the pressure of work, friendships, relationships and family behind you. Visualize your next conquest as the masseur or masseuse pulls, tugs, slaps, presses and rubs the stress and pain of life away.

You are a warm-blooded creature and have the primitive urge to project yourself energetically, actively and sexually. This puts you at risk of accidents. If you are charging around with your mind full of ideas and you are not fully concentrating on safety factors, accidents will happen. So be careful! You are quite resistant to infection; you may suffer from the occasional winter cold, but we all do so there is no big deal in that.

Future

The horns of the Ram are pushing you forward and thrusting you on to higher and higher achievements. Your future happiness is looking good. You are involved in a stable relationship that is working well because your partner does not let you get away with much and you respond to the demands your partner makes on you. You are aware that you thrive on change and you (consciously and unconsciously) create change. You will push forward and reach your individual goals, whatever they may be. Your love life prospers, and life in general is good to you.

New Aries, you have everything going for you and the future has never looked so rosy and exciting. Your life is filled from morning to night with enjoyment and you hardly have time to catch your breath. How the other, less active Star Signs must envy you, always on the move meeting electrifying challenges with only 24 hours in each day to do it all in! You deserve the lifestyle you want, and if you want it badly enough you will surely get it. Go for it, New Aries!

The New Taurus

Third Sign of the Zodiac:
14 May to 20 June

- Ruling planet: *Venus*
- Element: *Earth*
- Quality: *Fixed*
- Best Signs for Love: *Gemini, Libra, Aquarius (Aries, Sagittarius)*

Personality

Venus, the ruling planet for the New Taurean, makes a big difference from boring old Mercury (ruling planet for most of you under the 'old' Zodiac). Yes, you are still steadfast and reliable, but you are not like the Roman god Janus, two-faced and superficial. There is no doubt that you like to be secure and you feel safe with things and people that you can trust. You often seek the opinions of others in an effort to test them – to see if they are 'with you'. You need to know – and once you do, you relax. Creature comforts and inactivity are really your strengths. You look at life in a typical Fixed Earth Sign way, 'sitting on the fence' and 'not wanting to get involved'.

Your old Air Sign linked with Mercury suggested you were a gossip-monger – forget it. You are happy to be left out of other people's dramas. As long as there is good food in the oven and something interesting on television, you are quite content.

Did you realize that Venus makes you something of a romantic (a quality not previously attributed to you)? However, you would never let romance stand in the way of a good meal! The New Taurean has one eye on the future and the other on ways to maintain a lavish lifestyle. You are always realistic in your goals because you reflect on what can be achieved. This comes from your 'Negative' Sign. When astrologers use the term 'Negative' we tend to mean 'introverted' – though not in the social sense but in the way you draw energy from deep within yourself. You are not really ambitious because you know what you can realistically achieve. You know your limitations. You do not seek fame. You manage to keep yourself going and comfortably maintained. You value simplicity, but life in the twentieth century is not simple and, as a result, you often fail to see the wider picture. If you cannot see it in front of you, then for you it does not exist, which means you sometimes miss out on the nuances of life.

The spiritual life is something of a mystery to the New Taurean. You are notoriously sceptical. 'If you cannot see it or measure it or touch it, how do you know it exists?' you ask. You have a defiant, hard-headed attitude towards things that are woolly and foggy. This down-to-earth approach has real benefits in that it keeps you out of trouble and establishes for you the parameters of your reality – it gives you the life you like: easy-going, relaxed and full of comfort.

Before you form a friendship you need to know about the person before you commit yourself. Ideally, you would like to ask him or her for a cv or a reference first! This cynicism is healthy for you, especially when all around are losing their heads. You will keep your feet firmly on the ground when those around you are floating off into the clouds of their dreams or ideals.

You are very sensual, not only in the sexual sense but in every sense. You like to look good and have a flair for fashion and colour co-ordination. You love to feel and to touch. You are a tactile individual; the texture of certain types of material thrills you. Silk underwear, satin-soft sheets, delicate sensual materials – mmm! This fetish of yours is all part of your desire to be comfortable. The Taurus symbol resembles the full face and horns of the bull and represents a powerful build, a possessive animal and one with strength of character, who would, if under attack, respond with unflinching rage. Yes, you can resort to violence, partly because you fail to see the different facets to an argument.

You do like the good life: fine foods, nice clothes – but do watch your weight! Over-indulgence and lack of exercise can lead to a little flab. (Of course, you are not 'floppy' – you are quite solid.) You know all the best restaurants and you visit them as often as you can. Your tastes are rather conventional, though quality is also important to you. Your sensitivity stretches to your nose and you can smell a good dish from a mile away. Only the best fragrances will do for you; nothing cheap or nasty, for you the expensive perfumes that do not bowl you over but linger

like a summer flower scintillating in the background
– a bit like yourself, really. You also like a good car.
Nothing flashy or sporty, but a Volvo or Saab would
do very nicely – a solid vehicle to match your force-
ful frame.

You are in favour of tradition and your love of
beauty leads you to an appreciation of fine antiques
and well-made artefacts that have value. Your own
environment is most Epicurean: comfortable chairs,
good wine glasses, soft, luxuriant fabrics. You are a
collector or, let's face it, a bit of a hoarder. You like to
save your money and because you buy quality items
you do look after them and keep them in mint condition. Life is terribly simple: there are no shades of
grey, just black and white. The people you like are
'good', the ones you do not like are 'bad'. There is no
in between. You can see no subtleties.

So what, New Taurean? What is wrong with aban-
doning yourself in your pleasures? You have much to
offer with your philosophy, and some of those with
more angst-ridden Star Signs would do well to try
and imitate your easy-going nature. You are a delight
to be with and I for one would love to be invited to
one of your dinner parties because only the New
Taurean has the sophistication and style to organize
and run the perfectly pleasurable social evening.

The New Taurus Michael J. Fox is among very
good company, and so are you: Janet Jackson, Eric
Clapton, Grace Jones and Paul McCartney to name
but four. Michael is a fine example of the New
Taurean, with his love of tradition and his weird
blend of conservatism and sensuality. In common
with his fellow New Taureans, he loves to be sur-
rounded by beauty, which includes beautiful music.

Michael would agree with Nietzsche who said that without music, life would be a mistake.

The tennis player Gabriela Sabatini also joins the illustrious company of New Taurus people. The qualities displayed in Gabriela's tennis playing are typical of this new Sign: physically powerful and sensible under pressure with a no-nonsense but graceful style and no cheap shots. Again we have in Gabriela great sensuality combined with a safe, stalwart character.

Love and Relationships

We already know that you are very sensual and possessive and, as you bear the Sign of the Bull, you are powerful. Yes, powerful physically but also in your desires, emotions and attitudes. Your ruling planet is Venus, enabling you to demonstrate expressions of romance. Not a wild, stormy romance but a more conventional one where the correct protocol and proper rules of courtship are adhered to. In reality this approach is not very romantic at all – well, not until you are sure that you want to make a commitment. Before you feel able to do this, you feel you must know your partner well, know exactly who he or she is. You do not want many relationships. You simply want to find a good relationship with the right partner. When you do, my word, you will celebrate with the wedding of the year, after a suitable and properly long engagement. A white wedding with six bridesmaids, top hat and tails for the groom and perhaps a horse-drawn carriage to transport you to the reception. A small coastal village in southern France for your honeymoon...and so to bed!

Relationships for the New Taurean can lead to unforeseen danger. Because of your nature you are trusting and do not expect your partner ever to deceive you. You believe your partner when he or she says 'I love you.' It is all so black and white. Emotional blackmail and unconscious hostilities go unnoticed and until your partner says 'we are through' you have no idea that anything is wrong. You miss spotting the forces that are building up underneath, deep down. It does take a lot to get you angry. Your easy-going nature and endless patience are blessings. However, if you are pushed too far, then others had better beware, for the bull will charge. Your lack of subtlety inhibits any mastery of sarcasm or verbal abuse. You are not a manipulator. The only course of action open to you is physical. Dinner plates, your partner's favourite clothes or personal possessions, they all go in turn, broken to pieces and destroyed. There's nothing else for you to do but to charge once you have seen the red rag and anyone who stands in your way had better take cover.

A New Taurean client, Judith, sought my advice not too long ago. Her lover had taken a long weekend away from her, to think over their relationship. He couldn't understand, and had grown weary of, Judith's angry outbursts. Three complete sets of expensive dinner plates, cups and saucers had been smashed by her in uncontrollable rages of passion. She'd discovered that her partner had been staying over at a friend's house when he took regular business trips away. Judith had assumed her lover's friend to be male (as a New Taurean she of course saw everything in a black-and-white, conventional light). It had turned out that the friend was female. When Judith found out, the bull had charged with horns pointing down, ready to kill.

'Do you think your lover has been unfaithful to you?' I asked. 'Did he keep the gender of his friend secret from you?' 'Well, no. He didn't,' replied Judith. 'So what is the problem?' Judith had assumed too much and her assumptions were all based on boring social convention. As a New Taurean, she could not recognize an innocent, platonic friendship between her partner and a woman. Her own view of how personal relationships should be had clouded her vision. Staying overnight in a woman friend's house did not constitute unfaithfulness. I explained that her viewpoint was not unusual and that all New Taurus people share this characteristic with her. I advised that she and her partner go and visit this friend, so she could see for herself how it was. If she did not do this, I felt sure that her relationship would not last and she and her partner would have no future together. Judith made the visit and it turned out that her partner's friend was already involved in a relationship but that her lover worked away a lot of the time. He was, however, there when Judith and her partner called to see them. Everything is now fine and Judith has since been trying her best to interpret behaviour in a more analytical way (though her partner still sometimes has to hide the crockery!)

The sexual side of your relationship often takes priority. You are a sensual creature and where there is good sex, there you will remain. You do not take the moral high ground, saying that you are staying with one partner because you are virtuous, but you do like others to think this of you. The truth is, believe me, if the sex were bad you would soon be looking for a different relationship. When you choose to be faithful, you are. But beware! If you stray and gain sexual gratification elsewhere and try to keep it secret while supporting another relationship, you will be found out. You are not subtle enough to hide your secret delights and pleasures. Yet no other Star Sign can beat you for loyalty, fidelity and harmony once you have found what you want and the person you want. Unlike more complicated Star Signs, you simply want to be happy and comfortable, and for you that is not so difficult to achieve. You're a true Epicurean.

Your ideal lover would be a New Gemini, a New Libran or a New Aquarian, or to a lesser degree a New Aries or a New Sagittarian. Yes, quite a selection, but they would all suit you. New Libra, an Air Sign, would surround you and almost smother you with a blanket of kisses and whisperings in your ear.

Career

The Bull: strong, dependable and tough but softened by Venus and made passive by your introverted attitude. The civil service, where your methodical and deliberate approach to tasks and situations makes you the almost perfect candidate, is one option open to you. You do follow routine, and as a diplomat in the Foreign Office or an officer in the armed forces you would not be bothered by the trivia and by the minutiae of government policy. You would be there to enforce the rules and to carry out the mandate of the department you represented, and you would do so unquestioningly. If you were requested in print, in black and white, to ration water, you would perform your duty without question. It is no concern of yours if someone is thirsty. You assume somebody else will be looking after the welfare side of things. That is their problem. You perform your task in the proper manner.

Your thought processes follow accepted, reliable patterns. You are trustworthy and responsible, especially where a sense of material value needs to be exercised and where viable practicalities need to be enforced. If there is no risk of sudden change and if perseverance and patience are what's called for, who better than a New Taurean?

As an architect, banker, accountant or general administrator you would excel. Choose any one of these professions. If you are artistically inclined, your sensuality will find an outlet as a sculptor or with a 'hands on', expressive art.

Financially you are a saver and a hoarder. You will live very comfortably but you will not spend more than is strictly necessary if you can help it. Being the sensible type, you will have plenty in the bank with some extra put aside for a rainy day. You agree with W. Somerset Maugham, who said, 'Money is like a sixth sense without which you cannot make complete use of the other five.'

Health

Yes, you are inclined to be a little self-indulgent. Not for you, dieting and self-sacrifice. No, your ideal is to lie back and indulge yourself. One problem with this can be that you may be prone to weight problems. It is important that you take this information on board and work out a keep-fit strategy to ensure you are in tip-top condition. You like routine and are good at planning and sticking to rules. Here we go: draw up an exercise programme. Walk at least two miles a day (*yes*, two miles). Forget the Jaguar. Leave your car at home and take to your feet. Take just enough exercise to keep those extra inches away. And try to watch your diet. I know you eat mostly good, healthy foods, but those second helpings must cease.

It may be a myth to say that those who suffer from gout do so because of a rich lifestyle. However, you are prone to gout through lack of exercise and over-indulgence, so take care. The other ailment that you need to be wary of is infection of the throat. Forget all that suffering from rheumatism and asthma that was associated with your old Star Sign. Now you know you are prone to sore throats (though you probably know this already).

New Taurean, you are a warm-blooded creature and, apart from your vulnerable areas, you are quite a healthy person. The Bull is staunch and strong.

Future

What a rosy future lies ahead of you! A pleasant job, which finds you sitting behind a large desk and taking advantage of the traditional subsidized staff restaurant. Your house: cosy and warm, with all your favourite things and people near you. Your bank account accruing interest at a high rate; everything safe and solid. You and your partner are having a wonderful relationship and you are as happy as a bull home to the stable for the night. Sheer bliss!

But wait just a minute, and think about your lover. He or she may want a little more excitement out of life. You can provide it without spoiling your cosy, homely world. New Taurean, take a break! Occasionally, move away from the routine and splash out. Modify your habitual patterns. This will not disrupt you too much, but it will thrill your partner – and when you do settle back into the routine, how your partner will appreciate, spoil and cuddle you! You are lucky, New Taurean. Your future and your world are richly rewarding in every sense.

The New Gemini

*Fourth Sign of the Zodiac:
21 June to 19 July*

- Ruling planet: *Mercury*
- Element: *Air*
- Quality: *Mutable*
- Best Signs for Love: *Taurus, Capricorn
  (Cancer, Scorpio)*

Personality

The New Gemini is a perfect mediator. Your ruling planet is Mercury, the communicator, and you are excellent in the fields of diplomacy and in any position which requires good debating skills. If I may say so, you do talk rather a lot, but you are always a witty conversationalist and enjoyable to listen to.

The New Gemini is a Positive Sign and this fits well with your rather extrovert and outgoing nature. Mutability also complements your outgoing nature and expresses itself by making you very adaptable. Timid and over-emotional? Not at all!

Those characteristics belong to your old Star Sign. Because you talk a lot and, well, much of it is just general chit-chat, this does not mean that you are shallow. You are more than capable of great depth and concentration, but at the appropriate time. You have a broad range of interests and it is not your intention to specialize and gain in-depth knowledge of any one subject or thing. You have a spectrum of interests and ideas. You are symbolically represented by the Twins, which remind us that no two minds are alike. You have the advantage of a special duality which enables you to express yourself through your varied interests and hobbies. You are interested in events of the moment and in the latest gossip. You are not absent-minded, nor is your vision misty, but you are distracted easily because so many interesting things catch your attention. Life is a moving stream of people and interests, and you like to move with it.

The New Geminian treasures the capacity to think. You strongly believe in the right to make your own decisions and to form your own ideas. You get immense pleasure out of discovering something for yourself – this is your secret to success. You are well informed and it would be hard to fool you or to manipulate you emotionally. You are also a 'people person'. You genuinely like other people and are interested in them. You really want to know what makes them tick. Typically, you will talk to just about anyone. You make an ideal companion on long train journeys. If you sit next to a stranger, it will not be long before you are engrossed in conversation about anything and everything. You are one of the most open of all the Star Signs. On the other hand, because you tend to skim the surface of life, even though you have an amazing variety of life experiences, your capacity for relating deeply is forfeited. You spread yourself too thinly to allow you to get very close to people. No, you are not superficial, but there is an element of this within you. You have a wide circle of friends and acquaintances and, though you talk a lot, your conversation is not deeply emotional. Sometimes, when a conversation turns serious, you will make a joke and disappear!

With all those facts and fictions inside your head, and after all those life stories you've discussed, one would expect that your perception of yourself would be realistic. Unfortunately not. You are one of the least introspective of all the Star Signs. It will take a drama or some severe turmoil in your life before you will sit down and look at yourself. You do not care for responsibility, but you do deal with other people fairly. In a sense, you are an idealist and you have little sense of duty. You need mental and emotional mobility. You need lots of people in your life and lots of travel. Your mind is full of clutter, as is your life generally. You find language stimulating (and this relates to your ruler, Mercury). It is language that enables you and other New Geminians to be expressive – and you certainly are self-expressive. Not because you are egocentric but because you are genuinely fascinated by words and what they can do. You see words as tools, as a means of entry into the personality behind a face. 'There are many different language games to be played,' as the philosopher Wittgenstein said, and the New Geminian plays them all. You are a natural at languages and, if you have had the opportunity, I wouldn't be surprised if you could speak at least two languages other than your mother-tongue.

Life is not a serious business for you and you tend to drift, uncertain of where your skills and your interests lie. You decide on one course of action and then are almost immediately distracted by something new. Your boredom threshold is very low. You continually need fresh interests, fresh faces and fresh scenery. You are incapable of shutting out the stimuli around you, not that you want to, anyway, because your very essence depends on all that external stimuli.

Anjelica Huston, the wonderfully talented and versatile actress, is a New Geminian. She has always been determined to make her own decisions. No one distracts her from her planned course, yet she will allow herself to digress whenever she wants to – as long as she feels in control of her destiny. She is a good listener as well as a good talker, but she is more inclined to do the talking, especially if she is with someone who is not very interesting – and who can blame her? Anjelica has lots of friends, and is very happy that her life appears rather cluttered sometimes. The desert island certainly does not beckon the New Geminian.

Tom Hanks possesses the gamut of communicative skills characteristic of the New Geminian, and these skills have assured him a shining acting career. However, he also has the New Geminian trait of disappearing behind a curtain of laughs whenever conversations become too 'heavy'. Still, I'm sure he can 'get deep' with those very close to him. Tom Hanks (in common with Tom Cruise) has the child-like tendency to avoid facing up to any problems which are uncomfortable or inconvenient. But just take a look in the Appendix at all the multi-talented, interesting people who are New Geminians – they have a lot going for them!

Love and Relationships

As a lover you appear to be affectionate but you are sometimes concerned that you do not always know what your own feelings are, let alone how to express them to your partner. Come on, New Geminian, be a little more expressive. Because you have spread yourself so thinly, you have developed an over-simplified image of yourself in your consciousness. This self-perception has never allowed you to look deeply within yourself. You are rather fragile and do long to be emotionally secure, but your nature inhibits you from giving vent to the sentiments that really matter to you. You are often evasive and you dislike being probed about your secrets. Yet do you yourself know your secrets? You tend to deny yourself the opportunity to look deep within yourself. You will choose to take a circuitous path rather than face up to the reality of a problem. You don't help by setting yourself a high ethical standard and one which, because of your shifting nature, you invariably find impossible to live up to. When you try to aspire to your own self-imposed standards, you simply cave in beneath your unrealistic superego.

Your lover may find your lack of emotional depth hard to understand, because he or she (if the relationship is new) will not realize that you have not yet explored your own emotions. Let me give you some advice: when your partner gets emotionally heavy, be firm. If you feel too rushed, state your case. But if you are indeed ready for a deep relationship, your lover deserves the best from you, and you certainly want to give all of yourself to your lover. So why not just do it? Don't laugh and run.

You are elusive. You sparkle and bubble on the surface, but what is happening underneath? You have strong emotional currents and huge tides of energy ebbing and flowing inside, and you must allow yourself time (you owe it to yourself and to your partner) to explore these feelings. If you need help and your partner is understanding and mature, you can work through your feelings together. This experience will bond you, forging a union between you and the one you love. Comedienne Phyllis Diller once said, 'Never go to bed mad. Stay up and fight.' It would be so good for your relationship if you would just allow your partner to search with you, to travel on that difficult voyage of discovery. I know this will be the hardest journey you and your partner will undertake. But once you have travelled through the dry, flat deserts of the emotional landscape and have reached the oasis, you will know it has been a journey worth making.

A New Geminian friend of mine had weathered some real storms with her lover, who wanted her to be open and share with him a part of herself. Whenever he became emotional she would made a quick joke or change the subject, anything to avoid an open display of emotion. The truth is, my friend wasn't being uncooperative, she simply didn't know how to open up. Her life had been full and very busy. She had an active career and the opportunity to explore her own feelings had never really presented itself. 'Tell your partner the truth,' I advised, 'tell him that you do not know how to explore your deeper feelings and that you are scared to do so. You are scared of the unknown.' In this way at least her partner would be involved, and more sensitive to her predicament. Without her realizing it she had already begun the process of self-exploration by admitting to her fear of opening up.

I do not believe you are unemotional, New Geminian, but you are afraid to delve beneath the surface of your light-hearted displays of affection. The answer to this puzzle lies with your symbolic 'Twin' Sign, your duality. For the moment, let one of these 'Twins' slip away so that you can feel what it is like to be alone. Your Twin is not watching you and looking to take advantage like some irksome rival. You can freely express to your partner how you feel. Self-understanding is the key to all successful relationships, whether with a lover or friend. There will be times when you will need to meet your partner halfway, maybe after a dramatic emotional scene. Be ready for such a situation if you value your relationship, and be prepared to work to make it successful. Your flirtatious nature needs to be curbed when you are involved with someone who really loves you.

Your ideal partner would be a New Taurean or a New Capricornian and, to a lesser extent, a New Cancerian or a New Scorpio. Don't look so surprised! Believe me, these Star Signs would really work well for you and complement your own personality. The New Scorpio, for example, has a depth that would really uncover your darkest secrets and release you from shying away from your emotions. The New

Taurean would similarly get right to the heart of you, and you would welcome the strength and solidity of such a partner.

Career

The New Geminian has the gift of language and is mentally agile, an orator, a conversationalist. You should look for an outlet for these communication skills. You possess a primitive, almost chameleon-like ability to adjust yourself to your environment, and you can adapt your methods to suit various types of people. Your ideal future clearly lies in the media – either as a broadcaster, a print journalist, or even an impressionist. There are New Gemini people who can talk on the phone, write a letter, watch television and read a book all at the same time!

Your natural inquisitiveness is ideal for the career of reporter or investigative journalist. Here your intellect would be exercised to the fullest and you would be able to make discoveries, see things anew, travel and continually make fresh personal contacts. All media heads of departments should really be on the lookout for New Geminians. If you do not make it into the media world, then information technology has many openings for someone with your talents. Perhaps an Internet navigator, surfing the world's information superhighway looking for that unusual event or simply passing bits of gossip across the world? It would certainly satisfy your need to have the world at your fingertips! Printing and publishing, though more mechanical, would put you in an environment where ideas are being bounced around.

Marketing is also a career needing people with good communication and inter-personal skills. Lecturing or writing would attract you, but only for a while. You would be too restless to do either of these full-time. You love to use your natural talents fully. Your old Star Sign suggesting a career as gardener or estate agent – don't you believe it! You are a New Geminian and the world is your oyster.

Financially you will encounter few problems, earning a good living. You have talent, and captains of industry (including the film industry) want it. You will spend what you earn but, as you often say, you can always earn more – tomorrow is another day.

Health

You are an Air Sign and your vulnerable organs are your lungs, which tend to be a bit weak. Respiratory complaints such as bronchitis and asthma may bother you. A moderately dry, warm climate is where you should settle. It is an ideal environment for the New Geminian. The twin afflictions of bronchitis and asthma are typical of the 'Twins', both very different yet intrinsically associated with one another. Avoid the city in the rush hour or when the weather is very damp or very dry. The problem is, you see, smog and damp weather affect bronchitis, and dry weather and car exhaust affect the asthma. You really are in a bit of a quandary. All you can do is to take the best precautions you can.

The modern way of life can certainly aggravate your vulnerable organs! Your other weakness could be a touch of rheumatism. You can help yourself by avoiding damp conditions whenever possible.

The primary affliction to befall the New Geminians is sheer exhaustion. This is understandable, but it can be avoided. You need to slow down, take your time and stop dashing around like some dervish. I know you find it hard to be still, but at least try to go to bed at the proper time. A good night's sleep will go a long way to preventing fatigue. You are very healthy because you have an active life, more so than most of the other Star Signs. You keep trim and physically fit. Mentally you are continually engaged and though other Signs would be driven crazy by all the babble in your head, you thrive on it and it keeps your grey cells active.

Future

You are a Positive and not a Negative Sign; you draw lots of energy from the activities going on around you. Your future looks bright. You have the opportunity to find a partner, and if you both explore your feelings together you can achieve a sincerely meaningful and happy, involved relationship. You are very good company. Your face is expressive and you cheer people up with your liveliness and interesting conversation. Your home will be full of people: always someone staying overnight, friends to dinner, etc. – a truly lively and stimulating place to be! You are lucky and your New Star Sign endorses the New You. Be yourself and you will make the best of your future.

You are a wonderful person, New Geminian, always on the move, always searching for new ways to enjoy and entertain yourself. What an exciting time you will give your lover, night after night, jumping from one adventure to another. But beware: do not tire your partner out. Not everyone has your energy, your capacity for change and tolerance of chaos. Give your lover a night in, sitting quietly watching television while you go out. The world is full of happiness and you and your partner should be looking forward to the future, which is sure to reflect the dazzling light that shines from your heart!

The New Cancer

Fifth Sign of the Zodiac:
20 July to 19 August

- Ruling planet: *Moon*
- Element: *Water*
- Quality: *Cardinal*
- Best Signs for Love: *Leo, Sagittarius*
  (Gemini, Aquarius)

Personality

The need to feel a continuity with the past, especially
your own past, is very important to the New Cancerian. Your ruling 'planet' is the Moon, Earth's natural satellite, whose principle of rhythms and cycles
inspires you to ebb and flow with the rhythm of
nature. The Moon also affects your thought processes,
making you one of life's great thinkers. You have often
reflected on the fact that the circle never ends – it goes
around and around, returning to the same point after
every orbit. Similarly, history repeats itself. The past is
often more real to you than the present because it is

safe, it is known to you and it puts you in a frame of mind you enjoy: secure and safe. Your roots are tree-like and go deep into the earth. This makes you feel safe to explore your environment. You have a great love of history, including your own history, and if you ever become cut off from your roots you are miserable. Only when you make new ties and put down new roots do you start to grow and develop again.

You are a Water Sign and Negative. 'Negative' in the way you draw your energy deep from within you, not negative in a mental or social sense. You are highly sensitive even though outwardly you give the impression of impenetrable self-assurance and toughness. Your old Star Sign profile of being over-bearing and intolerant could not be more wrong. You New Cancerians are nothing of the sort. You have a Cardinal and not a Fixed quality, which means that you are very enterprising at all levels. The Crab really does symbolize your character. If you desire something, you do not move directly towards it; you circumnavigate your goal and look as if you are going off in a completely different direc-tion. But when you reach your goal and close your pincers, there's no way anyone can persuade you to let go.

Your first concern is to protect those you love and care for. You are loyal to your family (both ancestral and present-day). You love to collect things and never throw anything away. Your house is filled with 'useful' junk that will probably never come in handy at all. But it is in your nature, New Cancerian; this action of saving makes you feel secure. You desire a womb-like shelter to withdraw to, with your collected things, while preserving your energy. Your

Element is Water, which seeks security. You love the familiarity of objects, people and places.

It is simply not true that you are manipulative. You possess a wonderful capacity for smoothing out arguments and bringing people together. This is not manipulation but an instinctive grace which you use and adopt in challenging situations. You need to feel needed, loved and cherished; in turn, you give love. Like the crab, you inhabit neither the water nor the land, but exist on the border between the two, belonging to both worlds and yet to none. On the one side there is the world of domesticity, on the other the ocean, the great expanse waiting to be discovered.

Without its shell the crab is defenceless; your hard exterior protects a person who is easily hurt and highly sensitive. You have developed a defensive attitude to protect your inner sensitivity. More than anything you fear rejection, humiliation and being made to look ridiculous. Take heart, no one is out to get you and there is no harm in a tiny amount of humiliation – in fact it is good for you. Suffering is good for the soul, even yours, New Cancerian.

My brother is a New Cancerian and, like you, he lived in mortal fear of humiliation. He was so scared that he planned his world around avoiding even the slightest embarrassment. One afternoon, he slipped in a friend's kitchen and fell to the floor, knocking over their rubbish bin in the process. He was mortified. We now laugh together about the incident and he is now less self-conscious and less fearful of humiliation. He admitted that this slight disgrace had been good for him.

You are a very special person. Your great quality is 'sustainability'. When others close to you are feeling vulnerable you can give them the strength and belief in themselves to pull through. You do this with such subtlety that those you are helping are unaware of what you are doing. Your ability to defuse the tension in a confrontational situation is quite remarkable. The Moon is a mediator and blesses you with excellent counselling skills. The ebb and flow of the tide, the emotional storms and rhythms effected by the Moon are channelled through you. You have an abundant ability to arbitrate.

Does it surprise you to learn that Arnold Schwarzenegger is a New Cancerian? It may do, but it should not. Look at how naturally he is able to play a fatherly (nurturing) role in some of his films, while at the same time being the epitome of self-assurance and toughness. No one is tougher than 'Big Arnie' and he is the ultimate survivor who has learned from the pain of humiliation how to pull through. When he migrated to the United States and won the Mr Universe contest, he used to pose like the Greek god Adonis for the rich and the vulgar. These people poked fun at him, as did the press, and made the usual remarks about 'all brawn and no brain'. This hurt him, but he had the strength of character (like you, New Cancerian) to pull through. He is now the highest paid movie star in the history of Hollywood.

Again, we see hard/soft qualities in Melanie Griffith, a New Cancer woman. Her role in the film *Working Girl* was exquisite casting, as it brought out all her New Cancerian attributes: the determined way she clung to her belief in herself in spite of apparently having the 'wrong background' for getting to the top. Like Melanie, many New Cancer people come from 'the wrong side of the tracks' and, on their way through the marshalling yards of life, are hurt by the insensitivity of other more loud, coarse and vulgar Star Signs. But your courage and tenacity pull you through and in the end you come out on top, not braying and shouting but respectfully and with grace.

Love and Relationships

The New Cancerian tends to be loyal in relationships. You value security, and anything that may jeopardize it is simply not on. You will fight to maintain a good relationship. You are a great romantic, very senti-mental and tender. This tenderness is a wonderful quality which very few other Signs possess. You can be emotional – perhaps a little over-emotional because you give 100 per cent to your partner and you unrealistically expect the same, which isn't really fair, is it? You cannot expect everyone to behave and feel just as you do. You may invest all your emotional energy into a relationship, but that is your nature, it's almost your *raison d'être*.

Your homely quality, the loving way you look after the nest, is really sweet. You are a creature of habit. You come home from the office, from a walk, from an aerobics class, and you collapse in your favourite chair with all your favourite things around you, including your very favourite: your partner. If either or both of you is in a profession that entails working away from home for weeks at a time, then this situation could lead to a state of emotional unset-tledness. I know that in the modern world you need to earn a living and it is often impossible to arrange life perfectly, but given your nature a job that means a lot of travel (for you or your partner) might really start to get you down after a while.

Being together with your partner and sharing time together is so important to you. The cosy, homely lifestyle is just what you need. You are very affectionate and it is here that your great strength lies in your relationship, in the giving of yourself to your loved ones. You do need to be careful, however: make sure your partner does not take advantage of you. You must learn to read the signals.The spoken word is not always the best mode of communication where emotional issues are concerned. Your partner's body language or sudden change of habit will tell you more about emotional issues than any amount of discussion.

You are the most faithful of all the Signs and once you have made a commitment you stick with it. For this reason you find it very difficult to cope in a relationship that isn't working. Indeed, you find breaking up a horrific experience. Early in a relationship, in what should be the halcyon days, you hold back out of fear of getting hurt if things don't work out. You need to be sure. Unfortunately your partner feels you are behaving coolly and that you're not really in love. We are back to the circle – only this time the circle has taken a rather more vicious turn. You withhold your true feelings, your partner feels rejected and behaves coldly towards you. This in turn confirms your belief that you were right to be cautious, thus you become more emotionally frigid. Your partner is fed up and cannot understand you. You have a blinding row and you become more withdrawn. The relationship is over before it has even begun! You lose out and so does your partner. I know you do not withhold deliberately, it is your nature, but you can try to make a bigger effort to open up, especially if you love your partner and are aware of the consequences of seeming cold. You must make a blind leap of faith. In most situations it will be worth it. If it isn't, it need not be the end of the world. You can always unclench those pincers and move on.

Sex is a tender, romantic and loving affair for you. You are very sensitive to tactile stimulation, so there is certainly some scope for adventure there. You enjoy the romantic build-up, the whole sexual experience, and although your lovemaking is somewhat formal, it is not at all boring for either of you. You could never rush straight into the sexual act. You need time to prepare and to make the most of the love ritual. Once you have your partner firmly in your 'pincers' you can be unbelievably gentle. New Cancerian, when you find the right relationship then you have a match made in heaven.

Your ideal partner's Star Sign would be New Leo or New Sagittarius. To a lesser degree, perhaps New Gemini or New Aquarius. Surprised? These Star Signs will work for you and, in a relationship, they would make you feel secure enough to vouchsafe a commitment.

Career

'Closing time, please. Let's have your glasses,' cries the New Cancerian manager of a large hotel or small country public house. Your natural ability to look after others in a pleasant and harmonious environment would make you ideal at dealing with the public. Who better to provide cosy, comfortable surroundings? You may not have thought of this type of profession before, but it would suit you down to the ground. You may have a hard, shell-like exterior of authority, but your soft, caring centre ensures that you come across as a warm individual. Working in industry as an overseer or quality controller would not be right for you. Forget your old Star Sign profile. Those occupations would drive you crazy.

You are very shrewd, intuitive and receptive, with a good memory for people's names and faces. These qualities endear you to people. By remembering their names you make people feel important. The simple error of getting a name wrong can deflate someone's ego way out of proportion to the intent behind the error. You never make that mistake. Hotels, leisure, the catering industry – any of these would utilize your skills. I visit the English Lake District quite often and a couple of years ago I called for a meal and a drink at a country hotel. Because it was winter the lounge bar was empty and I and the hotelier talked at some length. When I visited the same hotel over a year later, the hotelier greeted me with this: 'Hello, Walter! A glass of red wine, isn't it?' This is the New Cancerian. You make others feel good with little (but very important) kindnesses.

Financially, you are building up your nest egg. You are quite a good saver and you like to put by the same amount each month towards the future. You are never tempted to touch this fund. It's for later in life, for you and your partner, and it's growing year by year. By the time you are ready to dip into it, it will amount to quite a hefty sum.

People like you a lot and you will never be out of work, not for long, anyway – your natural charm will see to that.

Health

It is the underbelly of the Crab that is exposed, and it is your stomach and digestive system generally that are the vulnerable areas of your body. You like pleasant things and this includes 'naughty but nice' foods such as cream cakes and refined food products which (you keep forgetting) are only good in moderation. Eating these kinds of food at the expense of high-fibre, healthier options is really going to aggravate any digestive problems. Keep an eye on your diet. Is it varied enough? Are you eating enough of the right kinds of foods? You need nourishment that will pass easily but usefully through your system to keep your digestion in good working order. A high-fibre diet will 'keep you regular', and this is the key to a healthy digestive system. You are a creature of habit, so you will not find this regime difficult to maintain.

One other minor problem is your knees. If you are employed in a profession that involves standing for a lot of the time, you need to be conscious of your knees. Try bending them as often as possible, as this action lubricates them; or grab a chair and put your feet up for a quiet five minutes at every opportunity. There is absolutely nothing wrong with your back, as your old Star Sign suggested, so forget that. Your dorsal region should be fine.

You are a careful Sign and not likely to take chances. You are a home-lover and like nothing better than cuddling up to your partner on the chaise longue with your favourite things around you. This should keep you happy and in good health.

Future

The Crab is a creature of the water and of land. Building a nest and securing a world where you and your loved one can live happily is all you ask. Your New Star Sign is working well for you. It has always done so and the profile offered fits your personality like the shell fits the crab. I know you feel a little insecure because you now have a different Star Sign, but once you commit yourself to it everything will turn out for the best.

All those little pleasing habits you had but could not explain are now accounted for by your true Star Sign. The land and the sea are there for you to do with as you wish. Your future is looking great! You are a wonderful person and your partner is lucky to have found you. Your career and the social position you desire are both coming together, and you and your partner could not wish for greater happiness!

The New Leo

Sixth Sign of the Zodiac:
20 August to 15 September

- Ruling planet: *Sun*
- Element: *Fire*
- Quality: *Fixed*
- Best Signs for Love: *Ophiuchus, Cancer, Pisces (Virgo)*

Personality

If I were giving a large party as a token of my undying love for my partner, and I was worried about organizing it, I would immediately pick up the telephone and call you. The New Leo is a born organizer. You are not interfering or pedantic, as your old Star Sign indicated. Oh no, you are an organizer and an enthusiast. You are outspoken but it is good to hear what you have to say. Your ruling star is the Sun, a very powerful symbol which works through you to give you strength and the power of self-integration. You're the leader of the beasts: radiant, confident, full of fun and always ready to outshine any foe. Too modest? The New Leo? Not at all. Forget your old, deflating Star Sign. How could you be too modest? You are a Lion, a Fire element, Fixed and Positive. You are essentially self-expressive, energetic and assertive, with intensity and spontaneity. What a Sign!

Your life is open to endless possibilities, mostly to do with action, a challenge or fulfilling your own dreams. You hold on to your own ideals, and here a problem can arise for you. If your ideal does not match your reality, you become disorientated and confused. Whether in business, in relationships or with friends, you are baffled by the petty and nasty behaviour of others. As the Lion, the aristocrat of the jungle, you rise above such lowly behaviour. The intrusion of the small-minded and the tasteless are not welcome in your kingdom.

You possess natural qualities of leadership, but the basic conflict in your nature is indicated by the active Fire element and the static Fixed quality. The latter, luckily, is essential for your self-control. The Fiery, self-assertive element can become a little overbearing and dominant. You are always conspicuous, wherever you happen to be, and this does not bother you at all. In fact, you rather like it. But beware, there are those whose Star Signs clash with this aspect of your Sign, so don't be alarmed by their rather contemptuous looks or put-downs. You are generous, warmhearted, extremely dignified and broad-minded.

The Sun has so much energy, and channels that energy through you in a very positive way. The symbol of Leo emphasizes the lion's mane: bold, rich and regal. You are the powerful ruler of beasts; when you roar, all are obliged to sit up and listen. They ignore you at their peril. People frequently try to imitate New Leos. Who can blame them? You have style and charisma, and your sunny personality lifts people's spirits.

Nothing in the world is as important to you as your own world. You strive continually and you are an intolerable perfectionist regarding both your own activities and what you expect of others. You endeavour to fulfil your dreams, but if they are smashed you are not reduced to a quivering mess. No, the Lion's response to failure is to take a leap out of complacency and to strive again, with renewed vigour. You are able to laugh at yourself, which is a wonderful saving grace to counter-balance your streak of vanity.

You like speed and you go for the kind of vehicle that is showy and sporty: a Porsche or a Lamborghini. Well, you deserve the best, but just who do you think you are? It's obvious that the Sun is working wonders for you, but do you have to be so energetic and annoyingly pleasant all the time? Can't you just, for once, slow down and take a look around you? At least that would put you back in the same world as everybody else!

Some time ago, a group of friends and I were on a trip through the Rhône Valley in eastern France. Our transport broke down and the weather was bad. We were holed up in a grotto for several hours and were all feeling pretty miserable, when in walked a New Leo. Within five minutes we were all laughing. Our spirits had been lifted and the shadow hanging over us had disappeared. New Leos literally bring sunshine into other people's lives. One of you certainly brought some sunshine into my life on that rainy afternoon. You are extravagant in all things, including your personality. If you were ever down on your luck, you would in no time at all fight your way back to the top again. It is your nature; you are ruler of your realm.

Richard Gere displays his New Leo qualities in his ability to spread rays of sunshine wherever he goes. He is Hollywood's dream man and his smile and eyes radiate sunshine. He has the voice of a choirboy, soft and gentle. But when he roars he is a Lion and no one tangles with the ruler of the jungle.

And what of Shelley Long with her golden mane of luxuriant hair? She is certainly a New Leo of the very royal kind. Hers is a fun-loving but very regal personality; she has such zest for life that she could only be a New Leo.

Love and Relationships

Your loves and relationships are all very interesting but they are never smooth. Your ideals and horizons are too big, too grand and inevitably fall into conflict with real life. But while the ball is rolling, what a life! Love is a giant carousel, out of control. You dramatize everything: how it will be, where you are going, and what you are doing. You have the plans of a monarch: magnificent, expensive and unrealistic. You shower your partner with gifts, lavish in the extreme. But you cannot sustain the momentum of such a relationship, and eventually the whole thing grinds to a halt.

This does not get you down as it would other Signs. You recharge and the carousel starts spinning again, with or without the same partner. You are the sunshine of your own world and your partner tags along. It is your nature. Forget your strictly conventional (old Star Sign) self, you are anything but. As a lover you are sheer wizardry. You love with the same vigour you put into the rest of your life. You are in the fast lane and no one is overtaking you. When your partner tells you that the earth moved, believe it. You are that kind of lover. You are the ruler of your kingdom. You are a New Leo.

If you do make a commitment to a relationship and want to get seriously involved, you demand loyalty in return. A little flirtation, a little teasing you don't mind. New Leos enjoy a challenge. But the New Leo can be a jealous cat, and if your partner strays too far he or she will not be given the chance to do so again. You have a sense of honour, and when you are faithful you expect loyalty in return. You also expect to be treated like a monarch. But try to be realistic: the days of grace and favour are gone. No one is going to treat you like royalty, even if you think you should be. Just because the lion roams free in the natural jungle, you cannot roam free in the urban jungle. There are limits and boundaries which you must learn to respect. All animals are territorial, except the lion. Your nature has not changed but life has, and you must now stake a claim to your territory because the whole of the land cannot belong only to you. Modern life does not allow you the freedom enjoyed by the lion roaming free and uncontested in the jungle.

You do possess powerful and sincere feelings and you do bring sunshine into your partner's life. This is why you are such a likeable Sign. Everyone likes you

– even those who hate you (they're just jealous). Your personality is so big that everyone is hypnotized by you.

A New Leo client of mine came to see me because her relationship with her lover was on the rocks. She could not understand why, and it was hard even for me to understand why. My client was radiant and possessed so much energy and life that it was infectious. Her partner had left her, describing her as 'manic', and had still not returned after an absence of several days. He had left a few times before, but had always come back the next day. This time was different: 'I just do not understand him,' my client complained. 'When we first got involved we partied every night. Look at me – am I not glamorous? Am I not beautiful?' she purred. Yes, she was beautiful – she literally sparkled. 'Now he tells me he's had enough, that he can't go on!'

Her lover just couldn't keep up with her exuberant lifestyle. The Lion demands everything, you see. My client failed to see that her lover did not have the Sun channelling energy through him as the Sun channelled energy through her. She perceived her lover to be a dullard. When you are bouncing with energy it is difficult to see why others are not. I advised my client that if she really wanted to get involved with her lover once more, then she must compromise her ferocious social habits and consider his needs. My client is now with a new lover, the ball is rolling again and, with every turn, the excitement doubles: the wild, late nights get wilder and the partying gets more hectic as the Lion's whole social and sexual life is spinning around and around, utterly out of control. The more out of control, the better my client loves it.

Then suddenly the power may cut out, the Sun may stop shining and the relationship may grind to a halt. Trying to sustain the madness of such a relationship is almost destined to burn it out. One day my client will make a commitment to a partner, but it will not be for some time yet.

Your ideal partner would be a New Ophiuchan, a New Cancerian, a New Piscean or perhaps a New Virgoan. You need not be amazed – these Star Signs will really work well for you. Having a choice of four Signs from which to choose a partner should suit you as well – as ruler of the beasts, you deserve the Lion's share of love options.

Career

You have a strong sense of the dramatic and your world is filled with your own colourful characters which you portray when the mood takes you or when the situation permits. 'You ought to be on the stage.' How many people have said that to you? And it is true, you *should* be on the stage. An acting career would be perfect for you. Your sunny, warm-hearted, creative, artistic nature makes you an ideal thespian. I can visualize the hoardings: your name 20-foot high, illuminated by floodlights. The Lion roars and the audience sits engrossed. No acting role would be too challenging for you, whether Shakespeare or some backstreet sitcom. You would animate any character, making the part believable no matter how poor the script.

As a producer or director you would find fame, not just because of your creative ability (which you undoubtedly possess) but more because of your organizational skills. There is no other Star Sign who can organize like you can. Forget all those amateur prima donna directors who need several takes to get one simple shot. Just one take directed by the Lion and it would be in the can. 'It's a rap!' you would cry, and then you would spontaneously treat the actors and the crew to a slap-up meal to celebrate. You would not waste time asking the cast to think deeply about this action or that direction. The cast would know precisely what to do and where to move because you would direct them so perfectly. You have authority in your voice, and the nature of the Lion is such that those you command obey.

You could also utilize your organizational skills as a manager, company director, chairperson or social organizer. You would undoubtedly be successful in these roles but they might not be glamorous enough for you.

You will often be in financial trouble, popping in to see your bank manager again and again. You are extravagant and you spend and spend and spend. Only remember: buying the best for yourself and for others can be ruinous. Having said this, you will always come out all right – and in any event I am probably wasting my time asking you to show a little restraint. If you have taken the advice of your old Star Sign forecasts and have been stuck in what you would call a boring job – scientist, accountant, etc. – then bad luck. You now know which career direction to take if you wish to fulfil the Lion's leading role.

Health

With all your running and roaring around all day long, something has to give, and it does: your poor old back. Your dorsal region is your most vulnerable area and you need to take care of it. The first step, now that you are aware of a potential problem area, is to stop all that twisting around. Quick and sudden movements are not good for your spine or back in general. When you turn, do so slowly and not like a beast who is about to attack its prey. A very good preventative strategy for a weak back is to buy an orthopaedic mattress or bed. If, because of your extravagance, you're not able to afford one, then put an old door under your mattress. This may sound crude but it works, giving support for your back while you are sleeping.

The other, though less vulnerable, problem area is your circulatory system. You may already exercise, but the Lion needs periods of rest, too. Take note: there is a price to pay if you continue to burn the candle at both ends. The Sun may be your ruler, but there are occasionally clouds in the sky. Sometimes you need to take stock of your very active lifestyle.

You are a warm-blooded creature and do enjoy good health. The Lion has a tendency to shake off colds and flu more easily than the other Signs. Your strength of character and physique will serve you well throughout life.

Future

New Leos have a great deal of faith in themselves. Your confidence will give you the ability to follow your dreams. You may not always be successful (because you often set your sights on very distant and unreachable horizons), but you will enjoy the pursuit. Your warm-hearted and 'giving' nature attracts others to you and many people admire your style. You should be able to get involved in a stable relationship as long as you come down to earth now and again to give your partner time to recharge. You are half animal and half god, and you have not quite come to terms with this. Your New Star Sign will help the Lion, monarch of the Star Signs, adjust to this. Your future is looking better already!

New Leo, you are a wonderful person and your new Star Sign so perfectly matches your personality. You and your lover are very lucky and the future is bright (almost a supernova!) When you eventually make a commitment you will know that the time is right and that your decision is the correct one. You can have everything you have ever wanted, and there will be more and more every day, as the Sun appears above the morning horizon shining just for you!

The New Virgo

Seventh Sign of the Zodiac:
16 September to 30 October

- Ruling planet: *Mercury*
- Element: *Earth*
- Quality: *Mutable*
- Best Signs for Love: *Libra, Aquarius*
  (Leo, Aries)

Personality

The New Virgo takes in three of the old Star Signs –
Libra, Scorpio and Virgo – and is the most expansive
New Star Sign. More people are born under the New
Virgo Star Sign than any other. Big is beautiful. Those
who have recently joined New Virgo, do not be put
off by the name, it is sadly misinterpreted. Virgo has
little to do with prudishness and everything to do
with a primitive urge for perfection, for attaining the
pure essence of things. Your ruling planet is Mercury,
god of intelligence and communication. You are a
great controller of your emotions and if you examine

yourself closely you will become aware that many of your actions – for example, your almost obsessive tidiness – are really means of avoiding emotion. 'I must get busy,' one often hears a New Virgoan say. It is not because you have things to do, but because you need to control an emotion you would rather not face up to. You make yourself a cup of tea and pretend that there is something more urgent to be done than the dreaded task in hand. I know we all indulge in these diversionary tactics, but the difference is you are *always* doing it.

You are an Earth element and Negative – 'Negative', that is, in the way you draw on your own inner reserves, not in the sense of having a negative attitude. You are more introvert than extrovert, though your social skills are excellent. Your Mutable quality makes you adaptable and responsive.

Jealous, frivolous, shallow? Not at all! These personality traits belong to your old self, your old Star Sign. Forget them. They are not and never were anything like you. You are practical and are elevated by fine detail and by facts (Mercury). The other month I had a problem I was finding difficult to solve. I approached a New Virgoan friend of mine and she took the problem away from me, took it to pieces, analysed it, sifted through it in the most minute detail for a key to the significance of the whole and suddenly the problem was solved. This is how your mental processes function. My New Virgoan friend was an invaluable help to me, as I could not have solved that particular problem alone.

New Virgoans do need to be needed. You are not particularly ambitious. Your variety of interests means that you lack the single-mindedness necessary to go after a goal whole-heartedly. In many ways your nature is to look at the wider picture; you find it difficult to focus on one small piece unless you know what role it plays as part of the whole. Gambling is abhorrent to your very nature; if asked to have a flutter you would turn white with shock. The truth is, you feel that you never know when life might deal you a fatal blow, so you plan for the future rather than risk it on a wager.

Never far beneath your cool, analytical persona lies a rather sentimental romantic. You may appear to have a stern attitude towards drunks and irritating beggars asking you for your last pound (you would rather offer them advice), but this attitude stems from a fear that you, too, may one day be standing on the street corner asking for money. You sometimes cannot cope with the realities of the twentieth century, so you shut the world out in an effort to sift through and make sense of the many elements you feel unable to deal with all at once. That is not a problem, New Virgoan. It is in your nature to be analytical and discriminating.

The Virgin is the only feminine figure in the Zodiac, usually depicted holding an ear of wheat. In the ancient world Virgo was worshipped as an Earth goddess; this is where your strong Earth Element originates. Your unconscious process of grinding and separating in order to assimilate only the purest essence of things is something you find yourself doing automatically. You are trying very hard to knit the whole thing together. You do not feel ready to go out into the wider world until you feel safe in your understanding of it.

You sometimes keep yourself to yourself to avoid

personal encounters. Group encounters you can cope with: workshops, talks and seminars, or 'how to' demonstrations that have some relevance to you. Not that you find it impossible to be intimate and talk on a one-to-one basis, but you'd rather give it a miss in case it gets 'too heavy'.

Actress Julia Roberts is a New Virgoan and no one epitomizes this New Star Sign better than she does. Her character in the movie *Pretty Woman*, which shot her to international stardom, was perfect for her. A pure young woman (yes, 'pure' in the New Virgoan sense, in her raw, unspoiled state) is transformed into someone much more refined and sophisticated. Julia, I believe, displayed the essence of her own nature when playing this role. She is enormously talented, sensual and truly beautiful.

Another New Virgoan, and a close friend of Julia Roberts', is the star Michael Douglas. No matter what character he plays, the innocent essence of Michael's own nature comes across. Michael is also noted for his discrimination when looking for a part. He is, of course, offered hundreds of scripts each year, but chooses only those that are right for him. Like you, he is a New Virgoan who likes to sort out the wheat from the chaff. He then looks objectively at the whole piece, once he's understood how the parts fit together to make the whole.

Love and Relationships

Like most people, you will often seek in your partner that which you repress in yourself. Opposites do attract. You need someone who is practical and who will lift you out of your meditative moods. Emotion and sexuality are not enough for you; you require much more. Your Sign is ruled by Mercury, so for you there has to be more than mere passion in a relationship. A really successful partnership will include a meeting of minds. You are realistic; living off romantic dreams will not satisfy your need for intelligent conversation or variety. You take a long time to thaw on the romantic level. But, New Virgoan, wise up rather than create problems in your relationship. Explain to your partner that you do need time to fall in love and that you are trying your best. Your strictly conventional approach to a relationship – refined manners with a reasonable display of modest good-temperedness – gives off a certain signal. Often you appear to be in a trance, which your partner may mistake for the daze of a love-sick fool, but, looking again, your partner will find that your heart hasn't been touched and that love is something that he or she will have to nurture in you. When you are in love you need to be reminded that the key word is 'fun'. Love is not an illness – you are supposed to get 'the butterflies' when you think about the one you love. It's OK!

Love is magic, a laugh and one of the most exciting elements of your life. Try to recall your first love, as a child in the park or at the playground. Wasn't it exciting, that first kiss? You should not starve yourself of the sheer joy of life with your loved one. Saying you would rather work than meet your partner for a birthday treat just is not good enough. Enjoy yourself. It is not a crime and, in any case, think also of your partner's need to share happy times with you.

I had a client who came to see me last year. She

was a New Virgoan called Ingrid who was experiencing desperate trouble with her lover. They had been rowing and it finished with Ingrid's partner calling her miserable and no fun to be with. The perception Ingrid held of herself was, of course, completely different and she felt terribly hurt by her lover's comments. 'What do you do for fun?' I asked. Ingrid explained to me that in fact they didn't go out much. She was a teacher and needed to prepare the following day's work every evening. Ingrid was open with me as she discussed her problems: how she was feeling, how tired she was, what she intended doing about it.

'What about having some fun with your partner?' I suggested. Ingrid looked puzzled. 'Yes, fun!' I repeated. 'Next half-term, leave all your work behind and book a holiday away from the daily drudgery. Go somewhere slightly vulgar, a package holiday in the Mediterranean, perhaps. Get a little drunk or a lot drunk and make a fool of yourself. Just loosen up and you will find that you and your partner will grow closer together. You must allow you partner in, and one of the best ways to do this is by opening up, by losing your inhibitions and having fun.' That same weekend, Ingrid booked a table at a restaurant and left her class preparation at school. I hear that she and her partner are doing just fine.

Sharing is a two-way process. You give and your partner gives. You take and your partner takes. It cannot be a one-way process and I think this is something New Virgoans need to be conscious of when they are in a relationship. To make it work, let your partner see at least part of the real you. It will create a feeling inside that is very similar to the glow one feels when presenting gifts to loved ones on special occasions. You can be so busy in your own world, trying to perfect your world, that you become afraid of spontaneity and self-expression. Like my client Ingrid, you long to be free, to escape and to stop starving yourself of the joys of life. Put away the lists of things to do and the endless preparation. What are you preparing for? If you really must prioritize your work and create 'action lists', at least put 'have some fun' very high on the list! If you are currently looking for a partner, don't be too rigid in your demands. No one will match up to your perfectly delineated ideal of 'model partner'. Try to be a little more realistic and when you find someone you are attracted to, don't start nagging and criticizing if he or she does not meet every criterion. Be a little more adaptable and you will see before you trouble-free horizons. As I've said, you need to have fun – not all the time, but at least some of it. When you do, you make a great partner; your lover will feel really lucky to have found you.

Your ideal partner would be a New Libra or a New Aquarius, or perhaps a New Leo or a New Aries. Don't looked so shocked! These Star Signs are quite compatible with your own and would bring out the pure essence of your nature. You have a wide choice here and you should try all of them if you can. Your discriminating nature will tell you which one is best for you.

Career

If a task requires patience, careful analysis and lateral thinking, there is none better than a New Virgoan. You would excel as an analytical scientist, statistician, teacher, psychologist, technologist or even a private investigator. Your mental processes of discrimination and your assimilative abilities are fully developed, but they do need to be used – your brain loves exercise! Routine and very detailed work is definitely your forte, New Virgoan. Not the routine of the robotic and the mechanical, but of regular and recurring patterns. A sifting through of evidence, inspecting the smallest details, searching for clues – these activities come so easily to your probing mind. You are very shrewd, critical, practical and a good scholar. You deal easily with logical subtleties and in the role of educator your pupils would find you a most fascinating person. Gone would be the boring science lesson we all dreaded at school, where five minutes into it the whole class wanted to run out and throw themselves under a fast-moving train. When the New Virgoan presents a biology lecture, he or she brings the subject alive and makes it interesting. Your memory is good. All the facts are at your fingertips, so you never waste time spluttering and fumbling through old notes. The knowledge is already in your head.

Another good area in which you could make a positive career move is 'caring and health'. You have a strange curiosity about and interest in hygiene. I know you like a tidy house and feel that there is 'a place for everything and everything in its place' and that this trait can really get on people's nerves, but your fastidiousness does have real potential. You would feel comfortable in 'clean rooms' or any medical laboratory or theatre where masses of electronic instruments monitor the slightest change in a patient's condition. Who better to keep an eye on all those monitors? In an operating theatre you would be invaluable, the first member of the team to spot even the slightest malfunction. You have the ability to see things as a whole through your intuitive knowledge of how all the millions of parts work together.

You are not extravagant and you know how to look after your money. You have the talent to earn a very good living and your natural prudence will ensure you hang on to it. Financially, you should do well and acquire all the benefits that go with financial security. A nice house, a car (a five-door hatchback or an estate would suit you), foreign holidays (Florida, Switzerland or the Gambia), the lot. Money worries? Forget them.

Health

Well, you are a bit of a worrier, aren't you, New Virgoan? I really don't know why. Everything in your life is working out fine. You have a great life and yet still you worry. Your vulnerable organs are your intestines and the abdominal region. This vulnerability is aggravated by needless worrying. So stop! You of all people should realize that mind, body and spirit are all linked together. What affects one part affects the others. This is why when you worry, you have a propensity to develop digestive trouble. Nervous tension certainly can lead to butterflies and sometimes pain in the abdominal area. Nervous disorders are really your only concern, and can easily be prevented by lightening up just a little and by taking time out of your busy schedule to have fun.

You are a warm-blooded creature and very resilient

to infection. Other than the odd cold and flu symptoms, you are perfectly healthy. But watch out for those little aches and pains – those small twinges and feelings of stiffness. They are nothing pathological but are brought about by minor stresses and needless worrying. New Virgoan, you have nothing to worry about. You are having a really great life.

Future

'Don't put your cup of coffee on the polished table!' you have been heard to say. You and your partner share a good relationship which is working out really well – but do not get into a nagging and obsessive mode with your partner. New Virgoan, you are a wonderful person and everyone likes you. People want to be associated with you and the things you do. You love the pure essence of things, and your maturity and the undiluted way you view life reflects this.

Your future will improve as time goes by, because you will gradually work through all the minor problems which arise in your life. With your logical mind, you will see patterns emerging. These patterns you will fit together like pieces of a jigsaw until finally the complete picture will emerge – your whole life in marvellous perspective. With such a clear insight into your life and all who share it with you, your future will be assured. You are going to have a wonderful life, New Virgoan!

The New Libra

Eighth Sign of the Zodiac:
31 October to 22 November

- Ruling planet: *Venus*
- Element: *Air*
- Quality: *Cardinal*
- Best Signs for Love: *Virgo, Taurus*
  (Pisces, Ophiuchus)

Personality

Your sense of fair play and your natural ability to spot imbalances in every kind of situation drive other people crazy. When people are making a simple point for the sake of argument, your belief in all things being of equal value immediately neutralizes the polarity of the dialogue. The New Libran epitomizes the scales of justice. You have a natural urge to balance things, to weigh up every side of a controversy. Your ruling planet is Venus. Forget your old, troublesome ruler Mars, an energy sphere of anger and war. Venus is much more 'you'. You are also an Air element and Positive. The Negative (introspective) qualities previously attributed to those born at this time of year was simply not right at all. You are essentially expressive, communicative and mentally active, with the virtues of enterprise and spontaneity. Brooding, resentful and destructive? Not at all! Forget all that. Your Cardinal qualities (enterprise and ambition) will stand you in good stead all your life.

The New Libran loves relativity. Being with others does not, for you, necessarily involve emotion. It is more an art of comparison, the balancing up of asymmetrical patterns. This is what really concerns you. You love ritual and ceremony and you sense strongly that everything needs to be equitably balanced. Be careful, however, when you are dealing in real-life situations. Life is not fair and no amount of balancing on your part will make it so for everyone. Some people have everything: money, fame, good looks, intelligence, good health; while others, well, nothing at all. Do not let this imbalance get to you. There is little that you, as an individual, can do about it.

Even if you are tempted to use your notorious charm to manipulate people, you will always strive for the fairness and equity of the scales. Symbolically, the scales are the only inanimate object among the Star Signs and they are typical of you: always weighing arguments, holding life in the balance, bringing people together and comparing them. Equally you seek in others the qualities lacking in yourself. However, you sometimes weigh up the pros and cons for too long, swinging from one extreme to another and eventually ending up in the middle of the road (which isn't a particularly safe place to be).

You have a gift for creating style and elegance (Venus). Wherever you go, other people take notice of and admire you. You were born with an acute awareness that people have different opinions from you and that frightens you. Frequently you will agree with a friend or lover in order to get him or her to open up and to talk more. Even if you fundamentally disagree with what has been said, you generally take this 'softly softly' approach. You would never say, 'Go on, do it,' but rather, 'I think it would be really good for you to do it,' and immediately you have everyone eating out of your hand. You would need very little training in psychology – you are a natural. You generate feelings in others of gratitude for your thoughtfulness, and everyone marvels at your kindness. At the end of the day, almost everyone is happy and you have gained their support. You do have a flair, a gift for being able to achieve what you want with the minimum of offence. How can anyone be offended by you, since you always consult others before carrying out actions that might affect them? You are a supreme diplomat.

The problem is that others who are more direct, and who do not believe a word you are saying, may perceive you as a chronic hypocrite and a perpetual deceiver. You have been known to smile sweetly at people and pay them a nice compliment when in fact you cannot stand the sight of them. You also agree with both sides of an argument: 'Yes of course. You have my full support,' then, turning to the opposing camp, 'Oh, no. I would not support so and so. Your way is much better.' But you must realize, New Libran, that you cannot please all of the people all of the time.

Loyalty does not figure highly on your list of attributes. For instance, you would not go out of your way to help a colleague just because he or she had gone the extra mile for you on some previous occasion. To you, justice and fairness should be exercised independently of whether or not someone has done you a good turn. However, you do like to be fair in all your dealings and you would always much rather pay others a compliment than insult them. You look for the good and the positive in people and in life. You are a great lover of the truth but you can appear indecisive, as though you have no real ideas of your own, only those of others. New Libran, you may see the hidden characteristics which other Star Signs miss. We are often more than the sum of our parts; your great gift is that you see the good, the beauty and the truth in all of us. You are generous with your praise and a truly admirable person.

If you have one annoying trait, it is (ironically) linked to your innate sense of fairness. You are discussing a topic over coffee; your friend has one point of view so you decide to take the opposite point of view. Halfway through the discussion you move around to support your friend's viewpoint and then discover your friend has moved towards your opposing one. What is the point of all this? I suspect you just love indulging in the art of debate. But remember, this can be irritating to some people.

Actress Jamie Lee Curtis has all the New Libran qualities. She is charming, easy-going and kind. All her colleagues will testify that she is also very diplomatic and will do almost anything for peace and harmony. Balance is so important to Jamie Lee, especially in the motion picture industry where her ability to rise above any pettiness or obstinacy is very much a New Libran quality.

International tennis champion Boris Becker is also a New Libran. He too uses his natural sense of balance in his sport. Often, aggression control is necessary and, above all, the will to behave in a cool manner even when the adrenalin is soaring high. Boris can do it. Many other Star Signs would lose control in tense situations – but not Boris. He uses his talent to the full by remaining as well balanced as possible, which is what gives him the edge. Advantage, Becker!

Love and Relationships

Yours is a marriage of two minds rather than the earthy mating of the sexes. You know all about relationships. You know all about your partner or your lover, and he or she will be the one who benefits from this. Be careful, though: discussing love is not actually the same as showing love or feeling love. Your partner may need you to be much more demonstrative in the physical sense.

You are a cool, calm lover who likes to feel in control at all times, and for most of the time this works for you. But you must understand that there are times when love is without reason and takes the form of red-hot passion – if you are involved in such a relationship you will feel quite disorientated. You need harmony and peace in your relationships. Venus is your ruling planet, so you can be rather romantic and you are capable of being a little flirtatious. Jealousy is not one of your characteristics, as your old Star Sign indicated. That old self-image really did create many problems for you when you attempted to figure out your personal affairs.

If you could learn to give yourself fully, holding nothing back, you would make a most ardent lover. The secret is to trust your emotions. You put enormous amounts of energy into a relationship if you know you've found the right person, and you deserve to get a lot back. You adjust, compromise and shift in order to be accommodating. It is in your nature. You also need companionship; if you are with someone who likes to be independent, then say 'goodbye' to the relationship – it will never work. In your search for a partner remember this: you like to be with someone a lot of the time, doing everything and going everywhere together. Your lover may see things differently, so do beware of this when choosing your special someone.

You take quite a while to offer your love, usually only after much thought and when you feel that you have known your lover for a long time. If your lover knows you very well he or she can gently coax and cajole you into opening up emotionally. The process must be undertaken in an atmosphere of trust for it to succeed. The rewards are great, New Libran, and you will find that your lover accepts the real you. Just be yourself; save all the masks for the world out there, not for your lover.

A friend of mine called Sandra, a New Libran, came to see me not long ago. She was quite distressed because her relationship was 'out of balance' and no matter what she did to please her partner he was never satisfied. 'What kind of things do you do to please him?' I inquired. She replied that her lover had said he admired Michelle Pfeiffer, so Sandra, in an attempt to please him, had tried to take on the persona of Michelle Pfeiffer. Her lover also enjoyed Chinese food, so Sandra had joined an evening class on oriental cooking. Her lover also liked watching American football on television, so Sandra had learned the names of the players in his favourite team and had pretended to like it, too! The list was endless, but I think you see the pattern.

Sandra attempted to be everything her lover desired except for the most important thing of all: herself. The scales had tipped and were in danger of falling over. 'Be yourself,' I advised her, 'because your lover was attracted to you for your own qualities, not those of some glamorous movie star. They are all a part of his erotic fantasies; if Michelle Pfeiffer moved in with your lover, it wouldn't last.' Sandra had failed to reach a sense of equilibrium and in her desperation had left her *self* behind.

Sandra and her lover are now back on an even keel. Their relationship has gone from strength to strength because Sandra has opened up and allowed her 'self' to become exposed. New Libran, take a chance and trust your partner – you may be in for a lovely surprise.

Most other Star Signs find it difficult to discuss their relationships because they feel embarrassed. Your trouble is that, if given the chance, you would spend hours discussing every detail of your relationship when there is absolutely nothing wrong with it. Your lover says to you, 'I love you.' All your partner expects and wishes to hear from you is, 'I love you, too.' Instead, you begin talking about Plato's theory of Forms and the ideal Form: 'Love'. Believe me, your partner is not interested. Your lover wants to love you on an emotional and physical level. Once you accept this you'll be glad that your philosophizing is rudely interrupted now and again.

You are considerate in every detail and lavish your lover with all kinds of affection. In one sense, you are the ultimate lover because your love encompasses your partner, your country, your job, your family, next door's dog and all of humanity. This is your marvellous quality, New Libran: your primitive urge for unity and to relate to others. But don't always do what you think is expected of you. Take some notice of your self and act on your own decisions. You are a marvellous person and have so much to give.

Your ideal lover would be a New Virgoan or a New Taurean, or perhaps a New Piscean or a New Ophiuchan. Surprised? Yet any of these Star Signs would work well for you. If you weigh up each one you will see there is a balance, a symmetry of types. You would value New Virgoan's self-assured way of steering you along the best path; a New Taurean would be strong enough to say 'No' on your behalf after you've said 'Yes' to everyone.

Career

Your whole life revolves around relationships of one kind or another. Your ideal profession should reflect this love of kinship: leading a workshop, heading a business meeting, listening to everyone's point of view and carefully weighing up all of the arguments before offering your learned opinion. You are a mediator, New Libran, and you are capable of exercising balanced judgement. As a High Court judge your natural skills would be invaluable, but courts are a little dull for your artistic flair.

You are in many ways seeking a sense of harmony. Your cheerful and compromising nature might push you towards the diplomatic sphere. Not necessarily the civil service, but any number of vocations: a beauty specialist or the head of a human resource unit within a large company, perhaps in the cosmetics industry – or in any sector where you are dealing with people or dealing with differences of opinion. You have a strong sense of social duty and like to conform in a practical way to community life. This can lead to a career in politics, either at the local or national level. Yes, the New Libran is a politician in every aspect of life. But, just wait one moment: don't go promising everything to everybody just to get yourself elected. Again, be yourself and maintain a sense of stability.

You are neither reckless nor thrifty with your wealth. You always balance the choices you have regarding financial matters: if you cannot afford something, you don't buy it; if you can afford it, you do. Your talents will always earn you a good living and you will prosper financially. This is good news, because financial security allows you to pursue your hobbies and interests, of which you have many.

Health

The most vulnerable organs for the New Libran are your kidneys. The kidneys are symbolic of you:

weighing the good against the bad and eliminating what is unwanted. This biological function reflects your mental function, striving for that fine balance so that you feel totally harmonious. You are neither cold-blooded nor warm-blooded, but stand alone outside all the other Star Signs. It is difficult to say what ailments, other than possible kidney trouble, may befall you. You enjoy very good health and are rarely unwell. If illness does strike, you will probably be confined to bed. The other minor point which I feel is worth mentioning is your lumbago. Ask your partner (as you possess the diplomatic skills necessary) to massage your lower back for you. However, this complaint will probably only strike very late in life, so do not worry about it too much.

Future

You look to the future, balancing your life with all its ups and downs, attempting to equalize and make some sense of it. New Libran, you and your partner have a very special relationship. You discuss your emotions and let each other know how you are feeling. You never let anything fester. Everything is out and in the open. Yours is a wonderful Star Sign and you are a fantastic person. Count your blessings.

Weigh up your dreams against your achievements and you will be surprised at just how well you are doing. New Libran, the only limits to your future happiness are those you set. Look at what you believe to be possible and what is actually possible. Do not set your sights too low. The sky is the limit. You can have everything you want. The world is abundantly rich and you and your lover deserve a little slice of that richness. Life for you and your lover is simply wonderful, and the good times are only just beginning!

The New Scorpio

♏

Ninth Sign of the Zodiac:
23 to 29 November

- Ruling planets: *Mars and Pluto*
- Element: *Water*
- Quality: *Fixed*
- Best Signs for Love: *Aries, Sagittarius (Gemini, Libra)*

Personality

'I need space to speak freely about what is on my mind!' cries the New Scorpio who cannot stand closed and stifled conversation which restricts breadth and depth of thought. You have an intensity of expression and a store of energy that makes it crucial to you to be able to say what is on your mind. Let's be honest, Sagittarian of yesterday, this is not at all like your old Star Sign profile. So when you really want to spout forth, you can now do so in the knowledge that you're running true to form. New Scorpio needs room to manoeuvre and room to expand mentally in order to weave ambitious dreams – but reality needs to step in if you wish to fulfil your dreams. The New Scorpio is not at all secretive – this can be taken as honesty and openness, or you may be censured for not being able to keep a secret. You would not consciously betray a friend, as your loyalty is one of your more agreeable qualities. However, you may sometimes share with others information that you probably don't realize was told to you in confidence.

You are now a Water Sign rather than Fire, and this suits you better. Carl Jung described water as the element which links the spirit within us all together, a unifying fluid nourishing all life in our world. It is true that, with the Sun barely touching Scorpio on its journey around the heavens, your Star Sign has been squeezed into just one week of the Zodiac and is now the most compact Star Sign of the celestial year. Compact it may be, but with such quality. The richness and depth of your character epitomizes your New Star Sign.

It is worth mentioning that your ruling planets are Mars and Pluto, which have always, even in the past, worked well for you. Mars prevents your 'old' Fire from being totally quenched. Don't let the Negative (introspective) quality of your new Star Sign concern you. You know, deep down, that you have always been naturally passive – not passive in any social context, as you possess good social skills, but in the way you draw on your energy reserves. In any case, the combination of passively drawing energy from within and your New Scorpio trait of explosiveness allows a fine level of inner balance to be achieved.

As a New Scorpio you will travel far because you

possess clarity of vision about where it is you are going. This vision stems from an inner depth developed through your ascending planets. You have the strength of will to see your vision through. Once you have set a target, you go for it, almost as if there were nothing else in life. Only very occasionally will you deviate from your goal, when your train of thought has configured a better path (Pluto working through a process of elimination). One of your strongest points is that you have leadership skills; this sets you apart from others. You can take control, New Scorpio. You like to take command. You carry an aura of strength which makes those around you look and listen.

Others like to be near you because of your sanguine nature and your self-control. The words you utter carry weight by focusing Mars' principle of vitality, making you self-assertive. It is your gift of self-control and your coolness in tense situations that rubs off on others. You have never been tactless or boastful, as your previous traditional Star Sign described you. No, not you. Lose that perception of yourself. Those old Star Sign traits – tactlessness, extremism and extravagance – really hurt you didn't they? They exasperated your natural sense of fair play. You are a powerhouse of emotional energy and found such comments difficult to understand. Those false affectations, recklessness and unrestrained garishness were never part of you, and your indignant stand is now understandable in the knowledge of your New Star Sign profile. New Scorpio, you are a wonderful person and you must learn to love your New Self through your New Star Sign.

The New Scorpio is passionate, yes, and you carry

the strength of your convictions. If you have a well-thought-out idea you do become passionate about it, but your passion should not be mistaken for extremism. Extremism is against your very nature because you possess self-control and can be almost ice-like when advancing your ideas. You harness your energy constructively (Pluto's converging function), having developed an idea from deep within yourself.

As a New Scorpio, you need a wide canvas on which to paint your many diverse interests and pursuits. You are an explorer of the intellectual and mystical worlds. You have the concentration to hold an idea and to travel with it as far as you can take it.

You are quite a different person from your 'traditional' Star Sign, which was often perceived throughout history as a restless creature riding roughshod over everyone and everything. You have the tail and legs of a scorpion, but your upper region is part human and part eagle and has the power, through the Scorpio function, to rise above those who do not share your views, but you certainly do not wish to stamp on them.

Your destiny is linked with that of the highest intellects. Many mysteries have been solved by New Scorpios, and you do like to uncover secrets. A friend of mine, a New Scorpio, recently won an award for high achievement in her college work. Like you, she was academically gifted but, unlike other Star Signs, she did not use her talent as a ticket to a free ride. She won her award by seeing her goal through to the end, and going the extra mile to achieve that goal. This is typical of the New Scorpio, typical of you. New Scorpio is a finisher, one who gets the job done. You don't really need to stretch your imagination to see yourself in this new light, do you?

A well-balanced New Scorpio woman is the singer Tina Turner. Tina is intelligent, sensual and emotional; when she is angry her eyes look right through you and make you feel quite uncomfortable. After a stormy early life she has certainly got her act together. Tina has been described the world over as possessing raw, animal magnetism. I attended one of her concerts in the UK two years ago and it is true: when Tina strutted her stuff on stage the whole audience went crazy for her. What a New Scorpio woman!

Jonathan Kaplan, the internationally renowned film director, possesses all of the New Scorpio characteristics: penetrating thought, depth of vision and desire to reach the truth. The existential and surreal nature of much of his work captures the New Scorpio nature perfectly. Shadow and light, contrasting but related aspects of the New Scorpio consciousness.

Love and Relationships

New Scorpios do not play around but are steadfast, reliable and have the strength of character to say boldly exactly where they stand in business, friendship and personal relationships. New Scorpio is not the type who moralizes about infidelity to hide his or her own playing around. You are rather vulnerable to the green-eyed monster, jealousy, however. Just because your lover looks at someone else it does not mean he or she wants to stray. You should be able to control your feelings of suspicion and distrust. After all, you show superb control in all other matters. Do not let these negative feelings ruin a perfectly good relationship. You have worked hard to find the ideal relationship. You are in love and would give anything for your partner's happiness, but you are deep, subterranean, and you sometimes let your feelings override your common sense – you have excellent self-control but only up to a point. You reach a juncture from which there is no return and then you hold nothing back. The sting in your tail is released. Watch out for this jealous streak. You may have just discovered that this is a characteristic of your New Star Sign, but you have known it was within your character all along.

You are steadfast in most other areas of your life, you know that. You want a loving and sexually gratifying relationship built on trust and understanding, but you can't always handle it. You have to ruin everything by your unjustifiable distrust. If you could just let your emotions unfold gradually, things would work out fine. You manage to do this with excellent results in every other activity, even in your professional relationships. How many hearts have you broken, how many tears have been shed over your outbursts and hurtful remarks? When you are fired up and consumed by internal conflict, you are capable of deliberate cruelty. You know exactly what to say and when to attack. Take some advice: you cannot keep your lover all to yourself, in a cocoon. If you can't deal with your possessiveness you will not have a long and mutually loving relationship. You will experience stormy waters instead, drowning in a sea of your own suspicions and distrust.

You are one of the most passionate of the New Star Signs, with strong sexual feelings. You like your partner to have an active (even over-active!) libido. You often overheat when you are near the one you desire. This desire is almost primeval in its strength and stems from an unconscious motive that seeks expression through sex. Mars, working through your sensuality, influences you in this. You can't help yourself: when you want someone you must have him or her. Your lust transforms you into a crazed animal. The urge to be 'one' with another human being in an ecstatic and mystical embrace fires you.

You and your lover will be happy because, New Scorpio, you are a extraordinary person in many respects. Those who have compatible Star Signs will be very flattered by your passionate love for them. Your ideal partner's Star Sign would be New Aries or New Sagittarius, or perhaps New Gemini or New Libra. This may come as a surprise, but each of these Star Signs has something very positive to offer you. The natural polarity of your Star Sign and these will complement your attributes and achieve a firm sense of balance in your relationship.

Career

Solving mysteries and dealing with serious matters rather than trivialities are definitely your strong points. You are a natural investigator and would be a useful member of a team, working with a degree of autonomy, perhaps as a detective. The opposites of science and spirituality form an enigmatic split within you. Both become religions when followed fanatically. You would make an ideal physicist or spiritualist leader. These professions appear to be incongruous, yet they originate from the same source: a need to understand oneself, the world and the Cosmos. Go for the type of career which will answer this need. Your traditional Star Sign choice of administrator or civil servant should be forgotten. The mundane job, the nine-to-five routine is not for you, not for one with your unusual ability and enthusiasm. If you have unfortunately been trapped in a career that is not of your choice, you have been following the advice of your old Star Sign and you probably will have found that your career does not really suit you. I suspect you may have changed jobs many times and have felt pretty miserable. Now that you know of your true capabilities, you can follow your destiny.

If I needed to hire someone to perform a complex piece of work, a task involving laboriously sifting through masses of data, you would be the last person I'd choose. If, however, I required ideas, or had a piece of work which called for imagination and inspiration, the job would be yours. You are an intuitive creature and feel ideas from deep within, emotionally. You are passionate and it is this passion working with your intellect that drives you on to complete the task. Often you are correct about a hunch when looking for a solution to a problem. Your intuitive powers combined with your formidable intellectual ones make you a great troubleshooter and problem-solver.

You do, for all your powers of intellect, let money slip through your hands. The best advice I can give you is to take out a savings plan or an endowment policy. This way you will have money when you retire. Think about what you are doing and lose your snobbish attitude towards money. If you don't, you will never save and your future may not be rosy. Do not play the stock market. Put a little to one side each month into a good insurance policy. At least that way you will have something for the future.

Health

Your urinary and reproductive systems are your weak areas, New Scorpio. Knowing this, however, you can take preventative measures. Your lifestyle tends not to be conducive to good health in your vulnerable organs. Your eating, drinking and sleeping habits are irregular and there is a price to pay for this type of behaviour. You have, to some extent, sacrificed security for freedom. Your mind is forever off on some distant cloud or planning some ambitious dream or intellectual pursuit. This neglect of the more mundane aspects of looking after yourself can result in kidney or bladder problems.

Your animalistic sexual appetite will unavoidably give you trouble with your genitals. It would help if you pampered your erogenous zones. Spoil them with hot, herbal baths, creams and powders. This will give you pleasure and help to avoid pain in later life. I am not saying you should not enjoy your favourite sexual activities (even if I were, I know I should be wasting my time because your appetite does not listen to reason). But you must look after the parts of your body that give you so much pleasure.

Your general health is very good. You are a cold-blooded creature and you do not feel early signs of infection. This is a point well worth remembering, in that often you ignore the early signs of illness. This is why, when you eventually do succumb to infection, you really suffer. You are not often ill, but when you are it usually means taking to your bed for days on end. Take this advice and be warned: at the first sign of discomfort, take reasonable precautions.

Future

The New Scorpio is capable of deep, penetrating thought. You are a skilful negotiator, and often during intense discussion your opponent can be swayed by your cutting, probing arguments. Your skills are useful in the right context, but do not become a walking analytical machine devoid of empathy and mercy. Reasoning power like yours is awesome. The Sun rules the daytime sky and the Moon rules the night sky. Use this model and exert influence on your intellect and your emotions. Do not let one become dominant over the other.

You and you lover are so lucky. Your future together is blossoming and your relationship can only get better – and it will. Every day is a new dawn and every dawn brings more happiness and a greater sense of well-being. New Scorpio, you are a fantastic person. You and your lover will have a wonderful life together. All your dreams and visions will become a reality because you, New Scorpio, have the strength of will to make it happen.

The New Ophiuchus

Tenth Sign of the Zodiac:
30 November to 17 December

- Ruling planets: *Jupiter and Pluto*
- Element: *Water*
- Quality: *Mutable*
- Best Signs for Love: *Leo, Aries (Libra, Aquarius)*

Personality

> *Richard:* What's your Sign?
> *Victoria:* I'm sorry, it's unlisted.

What a very apt quote, from Mel Brookes' 'High Anxiety', for the New Ophiuchan to use. 'Unlisted' – yes, that was the former status of your Star Sign. But now that we all know the truth, isn't it about time your true Sign was described?

For a millennium, Ophiuchus the Healer has been suspended in the Zodiac unrecognized and your individuality has been misrepresented, your birth chart miscast. Now is the time to forget your old Star Sign;

if you think carefully about the personality profile it offered, you will know that its descriptions were nothing like you: tactless, boastful and too moralizing? Never!

You are now 'the Doctor' (although if truth be told you are also a bit of a hypochondriac). Still, there's nothing too amazing about this when you consider that a large proportion of psychoanalysts have a tendency towards craziness themselves. Their involvement in their subject consumes them and they become the patients and not the physicians! Watch out for this kind of 'self-engulfment'.

Your ruling planet is still Jupiter and is now working with your new Star Sign. Your other ruling planet is Pluto, associated with the creative forces, working through your unconscious. The planets are responsible for your continuing expansion and growth brought about by understanding others; Pluto, in particular, is responsible for your powers of transformation and self-renewal. Ophiuchus is a Water element with Mutable qualities. It is also a 'Negative' Sign, in the sense that you draw on your energy reserves from deep within yourself. You are prone to be introverted rather than extroverted, not in any social sense but only in how you recharge your energy levels.

Ophiuchus, the Serpent Bearer, is depicted as a large man holding a serpent in both hands. The symbol of the serpent (originally, a non-poisonous tree-snake) entwined around the staff of the healing god embodies a kind of mediation between earth and heaven. This serpent-and-staff symbol is used by the BMA and other medical associations the world over as a representation of the healing arts. Hippocrates was the first 'modern' doctor; even today doctors swear the 'Hippocratic oath', pledging allegiance to Ophiuchus.

You possess a primitive urge to help and comfort others. The serpent, unfeeling and cold, gives you detachment – a necessary trait if you are to cope well with the sick and needy. You share your knowledge and give freely of your skills for the benefit of others. New Ophiuchan, you are a wonderful, comforting person and this is precisely why others like to be associated with you.

Boastful and inconsiderate? Not at all! These characteristics from your 'traditional' Star Sign of Sagittarius were so incorrect – you are never inconsiderate. In fact the New Ophiuchan is quite the opposite: caring, empathic and with a strong desire to help. Many New Ophiuchans pass their time building not only relationships but all kind of things, material and spiritual. You are a builder (Jupiter) and your talents for creating and repairing are gargantuan. You love mixing things together like a true alchemist: making potions, blending herbs, compounding chemicals. It will not surprise you to learn that many New Ophiuchans are pharmacists and chemists. And you do like to repair things. You see biological systems as machines and this view can easily translate to inanimate objects, both mechanical and electrical.

You possess enormous energy and have a great zest for life. Some time ago I shook hands with a woman I had just met. Immediately I knew that she was an Ophiuchan. I could literally feel her energy in her handshake, feel the intense power rush from her body to mine. It was a great feeling. You possess great inner strength and have enormous reserves of energy lying dormant in case of emergency. You have a need to protect yourself and others, however, which can be interpreted as inflexibility, austerity and a cruel nature. This is not true; you are a terrific person – but watch out for this over-protective trait even though it springs from a desire to help.

The Serpent Bearer is also a diplomat. You can slither and slide in and out of delicate emotional situations, silently and without being noticed. You do, like a serpent, notice everything. Your great empathy allows you to sense an atmosphere and sometimes what individual people are feeling. You know if they are angry, frustrated, keeping a secret or happy. You are often oblivious to social conventions or social status, treating everyone the same, whether they are princes or paupers. This mostly works to your advantage and leaves you free of airs and graces. If you are dealing with an odious snob your lack of skill in social etiquette soon puts him in his place and deflates his ego, once he realizes you hold him in no reverence. You do not do this intentionally, it is all a part of your Star Sign personality.

New Ophiuchan, you can be a little selfish. If you want your own way or are caught up with some work, then 'goodbye everybody else' until the project is finished. Yes, your selfishness does get the job done, but there is a price to pay in emotional terms, with regard to your partner, family and friends and even yourself.

Actress Kim Basinger is a New Ophiuchan and she too is a person of extremes. Kim is always looking out for other people and at the same time refusing to pander to the establishment. She has a marvellous personality and a strange innocence about her. She feels the suffering of others and can be very tender.

Another new New Ophiuchan is Woody Allen. Woody displays exactly the characteristics one would expect of a New Ophiuchan. He is the ultimate hypochondriac who nevertheless sees himself as the one to cure people of their ills. He is a self-proclaimed paranoiac and yet he has the insight to heal the world of its madness. He can be prudish and at the same time laughs at social convention. His numerous films, all commenting on our social situation, will keep us laughing and keep sociologists busy for the next century.

Love and Relationships

Do not let your partner walk all over you. You (the Healer) are not there to be used as a sponge to soak up everyone's negative emotional energy. Luckily you are capable of emotional detachment, but your empathic gifts may not be able to screen out all 'uptight' feelings, especially when you are seriously involved with your lover. You can be very intense when you're deeply in love, but when you are very involved with someone romantically you are at your most vulnerable.

You are naturally a very strong person, and your lover may seize on this inner strength as a source of energy for him or herself. When this happens you can literally feel the energy draining out of you. Your lover doesn't do this maliciously, of course not. It is unconscious. You must be careful none the less. Keep your detachment in this type of situation and use it; it may save your sanity. Your skill in sharing is so very rare and your partner is lucky to be able to give fully to you, because you provide a safe space and you give freely of your own emotional energy in a perfect symbiosis of love, a Cosmic connection. You can sometimes go over the top and this may result in petty and stupid arguments, but this does not happen very often. You have a great knack for making your partner feel at ease, and in return you ask for so little. But don't always try to be the saint; go out and get some serious partying done. You are certainly capable of having a good time because you are entertaining and a good conversationalist, and this is why your lover was attracted to you in the first place.

A New Ophiuchan client came to see me quite recently, feeling really drained by her present relationship. 'You look quite pale and drawn,' I remarked. Her partner had recently lost his job and he was emotionally very low. He naturally sought comfort from my client and because of her empathic abilities she took much of the stress away from her partner. He was soon feeling good, but my client carried all the negative tension for both of them. She had become really distressed and couldn't cope with it. 'You must immediately put some physical distance between your partner and yourself,' I advised. 'Otherwise you will absorb more negative tension and it will make you ill.' I arranged for my client to stay with her sister for one week to recover. This she did, and she is now perfectly fine. But here is the lesson for New Ophiuchans: when you feel that you cannot take on any more emotional baggage, especially that of those close to you, take some action to deal with your feeling of 'overload'. The way you immerse yourself in your relationships could cause a crisis in your life.

Your journey through relationships is like the serpent's path, full of winding bends and curves into different directions. You are, to a great extent, the most enigmatic of all the New Star Signs. You can be fastidious, often nauseatingly prim and proper when the occasion suits you, and yet you have little respect for social propriety. You confuse your partner when you make quite a fuss about a stain on a knife in a restaurant, yet during that same evening make an alarmingly rude gesture at a sophisticated woman who has irritated you in some way. You are so unconventional, but you don't care. So what if the next-door neighbour disapproves of your lifestyle? But these conflicting signals can be bewildering to your partner and others. New Ophiuchan, detachment and empathic gifts are at opposite ends of the emotional spectrum and you possess both. When you are empathic you are so close to your lover, almost in your lover's head; when you are detached, you are so distant that laser heat would not melt your icy-cold surface.

Because you are empathic you will know if and how deeply your partner loves you, and if you are both truly connected you will enjoy fiery passion. If your partner has any doubts about you, or vice versa, then you will sense it and that knowledge will have a cooling effect on you. Your journey through a relationship can be extremely complicated. But, New Ophiuchan, you are a fabulous person, a New Star Sign unrecognized for a millennium and you do feel this sense of injustice. Do not torture yourself any longer by denying your true status among the Signs of the Zodiac. Go after what you want with all the passion at your disposal!

Your ideal partner would be a New Leo or a New Aries, or perhaps a New Libran or a New Aquarian. This may seem surprising, but each of these Signs would be very good for you. Like yin and yang, where your differences are brought together you will reach perfect harmony. It is important you spend time seriously considering whom your lover should be, because you know that beyond that first physical attraction you need a more tangible personality to connect with.

Career

Fixing things (animate and inanimate) is where your natural talent lies. A job in the caring professions would be very suitable, but equally you would excel as an engineer (civil, electronic, mechanical). They two vocations may seem unrelated, but after all, surgeons are really engineers working on the human machine.

You could find yourself troubleshooting on the Internet information superhighway, or bringing all your powers of detachment to a difficult surgical procedure. If you have ended up in the wrong job – civil servant, investigator or estate agent, as your old Star Sign advised – it is only because the signposts along your true career path were slightly askew. I suspect you knew deep inside that this or that job didn't 'feel right'. (Where other Star Signs would say 'It doesn't look right' or 'It doesn't sound right', you would always say 'It doesn't *feel* right.' You interact with the world around you in this way.)

A refrigeration technician who came to fix my air

conditioning unit was a New Ophiuchan. He put his hand over the main microprocessor and said to me, 'It doesn't feel right, I don't think it's very well.' No matter what occupation you're in, you approach your work in this way. If you are working in a career where you really belong, well done! You will most likely be earning a good living and be well rewarded for your efforts.

Your attitude towards money is most strange, and though you profess no interest in it you spend much of your time talking about it. Often you are consumed by your financial situation – which, incidentally, is never too bad. How much money is in my purse? How much is in my bank? Has my pay cheque arrived? Don't be so obsessive with how much you have. Financially, you will do all right. You are working in your favourite job and earning more than enough to satisfy your level-headed lifestyle. Occasionally you do spend big, but only when you can afford it – and you know when that is because you can feel it, you somehow 'feel rich'.

Health

Most of your ailments are in your head and you often feel imaginary aches and twinges. Yes, New Ophiuchan, you really are a hypochondriac. Your bathroom cabinet contains more mixtures and remedies than the High Street chemist's shop. Your vulnerable area is your circulatory system, which connects to the lymphatic system. When you are feeling poorly it will be in the regions where your lymph nodes connect: under your arms, at the top of your legs. 'Perhaps all those little aches and pains weren't imaginary then; perhaps they originate here!' Just what I would expect you to say. The old joke about the hypochondriac's headstone inscription springs to mind: 'I told you I was ill.'

The way to improve circulation is exercise, so take some (perhaps walking or joining your local health-and-fitness centre for moderate workouts). You are a warm-blooded creature and, on the whole, enjoy very good health. Occasionally the strain of others' emotions can get you down, so if you feel washed out, put some distance between yourself and those who are creating the tension in your life.

Future

You close the door behind you. Your lover is already at home and you are looking forward to a cosy, romantic evening, just the two of you together, perfect. You settle down next to your partner and exchange the first embrace of the evening. The telephone rings and a friend needs your help. Well, this is exactly how it goes, so you're probably used to it, New Ophiuchan. Everybody knows they can rely on you in a jam and that is exactly what they do. Your lover is also used to this and knows you will be back soon. The Healer is off giving assistance where it is needed.

You are very lucky and your life is unfolding in a positive and meaningful way. You and your partner have everything you want. Your desires and dreams will be yours tomorrow. Your life is rather special and you too are extraordinary. Everything in your life is going according to plan, and you believe things cannot get any better. Well, they can and they will! You will be the focus of much attention now that your true Sign has, at last, been recognised. You will take this in your stride and are quite capable of enjoying all the attention you're going to receive.

The New Sagittarius

*Eleventh Sign of the Zodiac:
18 December to 18 January*

- Ruling planet: *Jupiter*
- Element: *Fire*
- Quality: *Mutable*
- Best Signs for Love: *Cancer, Scorpio
  (Taurus, Capricorn)*

Personality

Expansion in every direction and in every dimension
– mentally, physically and emotionally – are the qualities of the New Sagittarian. Narrow-minded and
too conventional? Not at all! Your 'traditional' Star
Sign persona (Capricorn) has held you back, New
Sagittarian. It kept you imprisoned and gave you no
opportunity to expand! Well, now you can. Even
those of you who already were Sagittarians will feel
better in the knowledge that your Star Sign now
offers you a more realistic profile. Those who were
Capricorns – no wonder you have been feeling fed up

with the descriptions of your Star Sign. You are now a Fire Sign and Positive. Introverted? You? You are always the first to jump up and sing to the Karaoke machine – the Fire in your gut and Positivity in your soul are responsible for this!

Your ruling planet is Jupiter, whose principle is expansion and growth. This principle does fit well with the new you. Your old ruling planet, Saturn, would only have held you back. Saturn stands for restriction and rigidity, neither of which reflects the real you. New Sagittarian, you are good at sports; you are open-minded and an interpreter of other people's ideas. The Cardinal aspect is replaced by Mutable, which is adaptable and variable rather than enterprising. New Sagittarius, you are not very enterprising, as you have known all along.

Friendship really does mean such a lot to you. Often you refer to your partner as your 'best friend'. You are not a loner and the thought of being alone scares you. You do need people around you to share your life (there is little point singing to the Karaoke when the bar is empty). You love to travel and there is a genuine streak of adventure in you. You don't wish to travel on some boring package holiday but to travel with a group of friends, perhaps hiring a car and cruising across the United States, stopping off wherever your fancy takes you. You are an explorer and you have a desire to understand life. You have an acute degree of insight and occasionally you like to become involved in heated philosophical discussions.

The New Sagittarius symbol has the lower part of a horse and the upper part of a human. This symbol combines the speed, power and other characteristics of the horse with the brain and potential wisdom of a human being. This sums you up perfectly, New Sagittarian: far-reaching, free-ranging, restless and possessing idealistic aims. You delight in new experiences and would be first in the queue at a new discotheque or a new and exotic restaurant. You have an intuitive sixth sense for what is going on, for where the action is and for what is about to happen. It could be the next big thing, in fashion, films, books, whatever – you will be in the know. You are more than just 'trendy', and as for those who accuse you of trendiness, tell them where to go. The New Sagittarian actually *sets* the trend and does not follow sheep-like, as other Signs do. You are no loser, you are a winner – and your winning, charismatic air rubs off on your friends, which is why they so like to be with you. Don't let some of your friends take you for a ride, however. Watch out. They know about your generous nature and may take advantage. You do have a remarkable eye for spotting opportunities even at a great distance, especially in the area of sport. You may not like to watch sport, but you do relish taking part. Outdoor sport appeals to you especially: abseiling, parachute jumping, bungee jumping. Forget netball or badminton, they are too tame for you. You would suffer from acute boredom pursuing such unexciting activities, especially because they are indoor sports which would give you mild claustrophobia and make your free spirit feel imprisoned.

A friend of mine, a New Sagittarian, was the first in her group of friends to travel on safari, to take flying lessons and to quit college. Oh yes, 'quit college' – so be warned about this impulsive New You. Look before you leap. Just because you are now free, do not throw away your future on some spur-of-the-moment idea. Then again, although you can be reckless you always seem to land right back on your feet. You are that type of person, but try not to behave in an irresponsible way. My friend, incidentally, came back to education after her two years' absence. She had travelled the world and experienced more in those two years than many other Star Signs would experience in a whole lifetime, meeting new people and making many friends. Friendship is the operative word, for making friends is important to you and comes easily to you as well.

Actor Kevin Costner is a New Sagittarian and typifies this in many ways: he is intellectually inclined, open-minded and deep thinking. He is one of Hollywood's most successful actors, writers, directors and produ-cers. Kevin is multi-dimensional, possessing untamed vision and appealing to women throughout the world.

Probably one of the most talented singers of all time, Annie Lennox displays her New Sagittarius characteristics of free-spiritedness, forever seeking new heights and having a burning desire to be the one who excels rather than standing at the sidelines of life. Songwriter, singer and video conceptualizer, all these qualities enable her to be where the action is. Annie is always busy with one project or another and her success has a lot to do with her originality and her passion for life.

Love and Relationships

The New Sagittarian has a great love for endless possibilities and situations which allow freedom and openness. You find commitments easy to make, but very hard to keep. This is why, New Sagittarian, you will need a good relationship with someone you really love and who loves you and understands you if your union is going to succeed. You will, even in a good relationship, be endlessly searching for new goals. This quest which drives you is the instinct of the archer, which pervades your spirit and your mind. There will be times, New Sagittarian, when you will want to expand beyond imagination and you stray off looking for someone or something different.

If you have a good relationship, you should value it. If your partner begins to nag you because you are often out having a good time on your own, then you need to get a grip of yourself because there is the possibility that you will drive the one you love into the arms of another. Pause for a while and take some time to consider how your partner feels.

If problems in your relationship arise they will definitely stem from your fear of responsibility. You feel uncomfortable if you are asked to be responsible, because it makes you feel tied down. Let me tell you something which will be of great comfort to you: you are an idealist, you possess a drive and a need to fulfil your romantic fantasies, yet when you are pushed into acting out those fantasies you will discover that they mean very little to you. You will always, in the end, head for home because that is where stability lies. You are complex: you fear all the trappings of stability yet you long for them, because stability allows you the security to dare to be adventurous and to explore.

Occasionally you will suffer from feelings of sexual

inadequacy. Being adventurous you find it difficult to live in a body which has limitations. Your vision of love is likely to be that of unrealistic romanticism: you atop a white charger, the one you love held captive, waiting for you to come to the rescue. But where do you go from there? To another romantic fantasy, of course. This is fine just so long as you remember that romantic fantasies can never be real. The pursuit of the perfect partner is an illusion which can never be realized. There is no perfect relationship and no perfect partner. Romantic liaisons are not made in heaven – so make the most of what you have in the real world.

Of course, there are times when you are willing to make a commitment to someone you really care about. That person had better realize that you need to be given a very free rein. You do not like to feel trapped. You need lots of room if your relationship is to be successful and long lasting. You will need to set boundaries and limitations in order to make your relationship work. Talk to your partner and agree a strategy, a plan which you can both adhere to. I know this is against your very nature, New Sagittarian, but do it just the same. Wishing to fly off on some quest, to escape the psychological as well as the sexual imprisonment and to feel the wind in your hair, is understandable – but you need to make some compromises to keep what is important to you.

You need to believe in something and you will always need goals in your relationship, even if those goals are unrealistic. If you are not allowed this freedom, then your relationship will not flourish. Yes, you are ardent and sincere and you do desire, beneath your 'devil may care' exterior, a degree of conventionality, but personal freedom is your god. Your best partner is one who will share your dreams and give you the space you need and be there for you when you come back down to earth. Luckily you are an entertaining and stimulating partner; you find life exciting and full of possibilities. Who can blame you for your indignant stand when other, less exciting mortals plead with you to 'grow up'? Don't pay them any mind. The world is one big fun-fair for you to play in.

Your generosity (both spiritual and material) is unbounded. But you cannot give freely or spontaneously. You never give when your lover needs you, only when you are ready to give, when it suits you. Be warned about this: you can be a bit self-centred when it comes to love. Outrageous tokens of affection are great, but do attempt to show *some* tenderness every day. It needn't be accompanied by some extravagant gesture; a loving word will keep your lover happy and feeling appreciated.

Your ideal lover would be a New Cancerian, a New Scorpio or possibly a New Taurean or New Capricornian. Shocked? Don't be. Any of these Star Signs would work well for you, offering harmony and intimate love and friendship. If you have been with different Signs and things have not worked out, you should now feel more confident to make a more informed decision. You are a wonderful person and you deserve your ideal lover!

Career

With your wide-ranging talents the whole world is your oyster as far as a career goes. Travel and tourism would make an excellent choice of career. As a representative for any large tour operator your natural talents would blossom, not only on the social scene (where you would excel) but also as an administrator. Your sense of vision would be an asset to any organization. Forget your old Star Sign career choices: scientist or headmaster? You would suffer terminal boredom. Can you imagine turning up every morning at some cold, sterile laboratory where you would be undertaking repetitive and soul-destroying tasks, while your adventurous spirit was crushed?

Your sporting activities may not be so useful when it comes to a career. You have never really been a 'team player', as this involves a commitment to the team and to the fans. A job as a coach you would not find challenging. You need to be *the* player. You are a player in the game of life, not one for standing on the sidelines encouraging others.

You would enjoy working with animals, especially horses (with whom you share an inborn affinity). You have a primitive urge to explore beyond the immediate and known environment. You need to understand things, as opposed to simply accepting them at face value.

A creative industry would also suit your talents, such as in the media (both print and broadcast) where you could be chasing one new idea after another, one fantasy after another, and all so far away from reality.

Marketing is another of your strong points. You have the ability to sell, to put over an idea – especially if the idea is new and you are in love with it. You would find the product sexy (literally) and that personal attachment, whether to an idea or artefact, would give you the competitive edge. If I had a new idea and wished to promote it, you would be the one for the job.

Financially, you will always land on your feet. You are a gambler. You see an opportunity and you take the chance. A recipe for financial success – most of the time.

Health

Your sporting activities and your adventurous lifestyle will leave their mark on your health. Many athletes suffer from hip and thigh complaints, and these are your weak spots too. Explorers, because they push themselves to the limit, are affected by these same complaints. Bad luck! At the first sign of aches and pains, take precautions. Don't ignore the little warning signals, the odd twinge of stiffness. In middle age you may experience a mild touch of sciatica and perhaps, in later years, rheumatism. Don't worry about this. You are generally very healthy. You lead a healthy life: outdoor pursuits during the daytime and indoor 'pursuits' at night. If you follow your Star Sign advice and do not ignore early signs of any problem, you will be fine.

You are a warm-blooded creature, strong, straight and agile. You do not suffer much from ill-health because you work at keeping yourself fit. Your old

Sign predicted problems with your digestive system brought about by worry and suppressing your emotions. Now you know that you are rightfully one of the most uninhibited of the New Star Signs – so have no fear of stress-related digestive problems.

Future

You have a great deal to look forward to. You are a free spirit and an adventurer in all things: mentally, physically and spiritually. From now on, everything will go just the way you want it to. Nothing will hold you back, and your days of frustrated longing to be 'somewhere else' are over. You now know what you can achieve, so go after it. You will be travelling to faraway places and exotic locations, in your fantasies and – yes, why not? – in reality too. Enjoy yourself. Enjoy your fantasies – they are now a part of you. You do not need to be shy of the New You. You're going to have a great time.

You and your lover are very lucky, sharing each other both as lovers and as friends. Your life is exciting and getting better every day. Everything you desire is just around the corner and it will only be a matter of time before all your dreams are fulfilled. New Sagittarian, you are having a great life and everything in the Cosmos is working to sustain you and your loved ones in a state of perpetual bliss.

The New Capricorn

Twelfth Sign of the Zodiac:
19 January to 15 February

- Ruling planet: *Saturn*
- Element: *Earth*
- Quality: *Cardinal*
- Best Signs for Love: *Gemini, Aquarius*
  (Leo, Sagittarius)

Personality

The New Capricornian is concerned about people's motives. If you were making a deal or making a point, or discussing a business proposition, you would not show 'the opposition' your hand. When the time was right you would throw down all your cards but one (your trump card). New Capricornians do not reveal themselves until they know exactly what they are doing.

Those of you born on the 19 or 20 January have remained with Capricorn under the true Star Sign system, but there will be subtle differences affecting your Cosmic profile. Those born on or after 21 January, welcome to your New Star Sign.

It is worth mentioning that your ruling planet is Saturn and this is why you are so good at meeting deadlines, keeping appointments and maintaining a conventional air. If you arrange to meet a friend, yes you will be on time for the appointment, but you may not be dressed for the occasion. You are an Earth element with Cardinal qualities, allowing you to be self-expressive and mentally active. Cranky, eccentric and fanatical? Not at all! Those characteristics belong to your old Sign, to your old self, and you are none of these. You are a New Capricornian.

You possess immense subtlety and always operate with an ulterior motive in mind, which gives you a slightly over-confident approach to all things. The problem here is that there is always one possibility you hadn't thought of, one complication that fouls up the best-laid plans. Never mind, New Capricornian. You can't have it all your own way!

You can legitimately be described as a 'concealed operator', or what is sometimes known as a 'dark horse'. You assess and make your plans quietly, out of the limelight, behind the scenes. Other, more extrovert Star Signs would be up front displaying their wares, believing they will take the advantage when the time is right. When the time is right, however, you are the one who has calculated all the moves, anticipated all the ploys; there you are, ready and waiting to execute your plan. The over-ambitious but less shrewd Star Signs lose out.

Don't be disturbed by that fact that yours is a 'Negative' Sign. 'Negative' simply describes the way you draw energy deep from within yourself. You are more introverted in the way you recharge yourself – you draw on your own reserves. You are slightly introverted in the social sense, too, but your social skills have never bothered you at all. You tend to regard most 'normal' people as brash and rather loud. You are the 'Goat', the symbol of which resembles a misshapen form of goat with a fish's curling tail. Mythically, this goat teaches the whole of humanity the ways of civilization. New Capricornian, you are so civilized. The Goat takes nothing for granted because you are methodical, resourceful and cautious. You have an inborn ability to suffer hardship, and when the going gets tough you are not defeated.

Prudence is your key note and you plan carefully, coolly and deliberately. Only one problem with this: you need to learn to switch off and have some fun. Trust your luck more. You are very lucky and, in any case, you can't plan and conspire to make luck. You do need goals, however. Without them you slide back down the tree you have worked so hard to climb. The world is a friendly place, if only you knew it, and if you are occasionally unsuccessful in attaining your goal, the world will forgive you. Trust me.

On the surface you have little time for romance. 'Romance won't pay the bills or buy the groceries,' I hear you say. But take heed of the words of Confucius: 'If you have two pennies, one you should spend on flour and the other you should spend on a flower.' Wise words indeed.

Your ruling planet, Saturn, is most concerned with self-discipline and channels energy through you in the form of a primitive urge to identify with the aims of your community and to initiate reform. You have a slight difficulty with human relationships, in that you like to be in control. It's certainly not that you're power-mad. It's just that being in control is for you the one sure way of avoiding that horrific feeling of being controlled by others!

If you are successful in your work you will develop deeper, more meaningful interests. You are a reflective thinker and your mild introversion supports this natural impulse. The New Capricornian may be drawn to the occult, where you can study the energy patterns that govern life, looking for an answer to life.

You are quite a difficult person to know. You like to look good, with nice (but not too flashy) clothes made from good-quality cloth. You feel comfortable only with what you perceive as the 'right' social image, and appearing to be a pillar of society really appeals to you. Again, you must learn to loosen up a little and take time out from your social responsibilities to go and do some serious revelling.

I know you are, for most of your life, planning to serve the ultimate purpose: fulfilling your destiny. All your powerful determination and quiet ambition have been working away inside you for most of your life. You have at times felt a bit imprisoned by your conventionality and you have occasional dreams of freedom. To buy land in Scotland and live quietly, working through the meaning of life, or perhaps to take to the dusty, red roads of the Arizona desert, driving off into the sunset – these fantasies appeal to you. Yours is a double-edged personality, making you all the more fascinating. No other Star Sign works so conscientiously, sacrificing everything in the pursuit of your goals. Deep inside you possess the urge to be the first. The scientist struggling for years, painstakingly working through laborious calculations; the poet stuck in a garret working by dim candlelight; the painter struggling unrecognized, producing masterpieces of brilliant originality; all of them working just to be the first, to be the one who advances the quality of life. You have dreams of immortality, your name in the history books. It is this dream, your personal vision, that keeps you working so meticulously over the years.

Actress Geena Davis is a typical New Capricornian: no matter what she does, she is always in a league of her own. Intelligent and possessing a serious, responsible attitude towards life, the stoical look behind her kind eyes tells you she means business. She is a romantic at heart, but she also displays the New Capricornian reserve.

Another New Capricornian is Tom Selleck, star of countless movies and television series. Again, beneath Tom's humour and easy-going manner lies a serious personality. Both Tom and Geena reflect the greatness that is yours, New Capricornian.

Love and Relationships

You are a cool customer, rather reserved, serious and faithful. You find personal relationships difficult because the Goat needs to be in control. When you express your emotions to your partner you feel exposed, and this frightens you. You have been protecting yourself (from what?) all of your life. You are often alone, like the goat grazing quietly. Your partner knows you are a romantic at heart, but gets a little resentful when you let your rational nature dictate to your heart. You would much rather stay at home on your partner's birthday if you felt that a nice meal in a restaurant would be too expensive. You are given to self-sacrifice, but sacrificing your partner's birthday party? This will never do. Safety and security are not everything, in a relationship or in life. You place too much value on respect and a sense of duty rather than on the pleasures inherent in a wild weekend of erotic bliss. You are of course capable of tenderness, but far too often you keep it locked away, hidden from view. You fear passion because for you it equals loss of control.

Why must you always try and take charge? Sometimes it would be much better to consult your partner and would certainly go a long way towards making your relationship more harmonious. You find it very difficult to express love and emotion in an easy way. If you love your partner, say so. How will he or she know if you don't let on? It will mean so much to your partner.

You have an independent nature and you can be dispassionate. You often conduct yourself in a detached manner and this coolness can lead to broken hearts, including your own.

A distant cousin of mine telephoned me in desperation late one cold January evening. She had lost control. Her lover had left and she was feeling very frightened. A typical New Capricornian, she prides herself on always doing her best, always presenting herself in the proper manner and saying the right things at the right time, to the right people. She told me she believed she was the perfect partner, forever looking after her lover's needs and sheltering him from the hard realities of life. I replied that she had in fact been smothering her partner, not with love but with a blanket of propriety, always worrying about what other people were thinking and always having to be seen to be doing the 'right' thing. I explained to my cousin that doing the right thing, so as to be socially accepted, is not what is required in a sharing and caring relationship.

'You are a New Capricornian and you really need to deal with those aspects of your Star Sign that make you wear a suit of armour plate,' I told her. We talked in some detail and eventually worked out a strategy that would 'equitably' make the relationship work. First, my cousin had to realize that her partner sees the beauty in her soul and was never attracted to her because of some silly social convention. My cousin had to allow her partner in, to give something of herself and try to drop the defensive shield surrounding her. I offered to call her partner, but no – she had to take control of the situation, which gave her some sense of security. The relationship is now working out well. My cousin rarely calls me these days, but when she does, she is after reassurance. Beneath all that armour she has doubts about her real self-worth. New Capricornian, listen to me. You are a wonderful Star Sign. You are a terrific person and you should try to let yourself enter into a relationship. Your partner is not trying to out-manoeuvre you; your partner loves you and wants to share your secret self with you. Let go – you'll find that revealing your soul can be one of the most rewarding experiences of your life. Keep your planning and scheming for the office; open up to your lover.

Your ideal lover would be a New Geminian or a

New Aquarian, or perhaps a New Leo or a New Sagittarian. Amazed? I know they are not what you expected, but these Star Signs are the best lovers for you. A relationship with any one of them will bring out and complement all of your natural (and best) qualities. Personal relationships, after the first passionate physical attraction, are all about getting along with one another. If we look at our friends and family we see that this 'getting along' can be quite difficult to accomplish. Knowing who you really are and who your lover is are crucial in a relationship.

Career

The Goat likes to be alone grazing by itself. Your ideal career should reflect this natural inclination. Your old Star Sign career profile suggested that you get involved in group work and occupations where you would use your (supposedly good) interpersonal skills. What a lot of foolishness. Those career paths are no use to the New Capricornian at all. Concentrate on the new, extraordinary you: manager, scientist, headmaster, business analyst or mathematician would all be ideal vocational options for you. You are a master of political savvy, weighing up the pros and cons and knowing exactly who is doing what. Your natural ability to out-manoeuvre the competition would also make you a very efficient marketing manager. One piece of advice: leave the personnel management and personal problem-solving to the human resource unit. You are not the person to deal with personalities, but you *are* the one to deal with the nitty-gritty of the accounts and statistical reports, or the complexities of business strategy and analysis.

As a scientist, your eye for detail and your patient, economizing, unemotional qualities could be exercised and developed. You carry an air of authority, New Capricornian, just by the way you walk. When you speak, your unemotional requests are taken as authoritative declarations. You are excellent at constructing systems of production and administration, where a rational nature is what is required. But take note: listen to others occasionally. You tend to be too narrow-minded, exacting and severe. Your colleagues may consider you a bit of a wet blanket. Be aware of your limitations and, when the need arises, use your calculating powers to feed the ego of your colleagues rather than alienating yourself from them.

Because of your astuteness you will not suffer from financial problems. Your old Star Sign description: erratic with money and a hopeless bohemian – you may have always liked the idea of being like that, but you've always known deep down that you're not really adventurous or extrovert enough to be a true bohemian. Financially, you are always planning where to place your money and how to get the highest return. You never trust your luck to fate and therefore take no chances. Yours are always secure and sound financial investments.

Health

Your legs are your vulnerable limbs, especially the knees. Your lifestyle does not help. After sitting for long hours at a stretch, your knee joints become stiff. Moderate exercise (walking is ideal), taken often, will do you good. Don't tell me you don't have the time – make time! With all your wheeling and dealing skills, you can wangle some time off.

You worry too much, which can bring on digestive upsets. Learn to relax. If the figures do not add up at the end of the working day, so what? The calculator will be there tomorrow. Don't be tempted to take work home with you – leave it on the desk. You must learn to channel your tension constructively. Worrying and suppressing your emotions will not help. You lead a sedentary life, and meditation may not really be the answer. Walking is the answer for you, so get going, leave your car at home and (if at all possible) walk to and from work. No excuses!

The Goat is a warm-blooded creature and the fish's tail is part of a cold-blooded creature. You are therefore quite a resilient Star Sign, possessing both 'cold' and 'hot' qualities. You do enjoy good health and are not poorly very often. You are one of the more healthy Star Signs.

Future

Because you plan, set targets, draw up action plans and leave nothing to chance, your future is all mapped out and secure. In case of a rainy day, your insurance policies and your savings are more than enough. Take a break and leave some aspect of your life to fate. In the end you cannot plan everything. You can try, but you will not be successful. Consider your partner's needs and add a little romance to your life. A little surprise adds to the magic of your personal relationship. I know you don't care for magic, but a little something special now and again is good and healthy for your relationship.

Your partner is very lucky to have you because you do take on so much of the burden of responsibility yourself. Your self-sacrificing way of carrying the world's problems on your shoulders is good for the relationship, as long as it does not get you down. You have a comfortable home, a good car and enough money to do the things you and your lover want to do. You are a great New Star Sign and a wonderful person. You can look forward to a fabulous life. A New Capricornian, nicely settled and planning all the time, you will achieve everything you have ever hoped for.

The New Aquarius

Thirteenth Sign of the Zodiac:
16 February to 11 March

- Ruling planets: *Saturn and Uranus*
- Element: *Air*
- Quality: *Fixed*
- Best Signs for Love: *Virgo, Capricorn (Ophiuchus, Cancer)*

Personality

The New Aquarius is one of the most humanitarian of the New Star Signs. You are all about love and ideals, about science and knowledge. Your main interests lie in the large-scale structure of social community, in the issues of right and wrong in society and on the larger international scene. You put intense energy into a cause and are often revolutionary.

The first few days of the new Star Sign carry over original Aquarians. Those born after 19 February, welcome to your true Star Sign. Your ruling planets are Saturn and Uranus. They channel energy through you, making you develop detachment, express unconventionality and give vent to an urge from deep within yourself to follow progressive causes. Touchy, secretive and confused? Not at all! Those characteristics belong to your old Star Sign. You are nothing like that. You are a wonderful person, an Air element with Fixed qualities, making you essentially self-expressive, mentally active and communicative. Now, this is much more like your real self. You are also a Positive Star Sign, which means you are slightly more extrovert than introvert.

Many of the causes you push are ahead of their time and, because they often appear to be 'far out', they meet with opposition. Your battle is not lost, however. The idea is subtly planted in the consciousness of the community and, once there, takes root in the minds of the less far-sighted Star Signs.

Many of the issues that concern you are related to groups, to society rather than to individuals. You have a really good sense of fair play and integrity. All New Aquarius people do. The Water Carrier is forward-looking and you are way ahead of your time. You will be found defending the underdog and the under-privileged as groups of oppressed people rather than in individual cases. The truth is, New Aquarian, you don't care deeply for individuals. True, you love everybody, but not individually. You promote public transport as a worthy cause, but really you don't like to use it yourself, much preferring to travel under your own steam, away from 'the public'.

You are also rather embarrassed by your emotions and regard any display of emotion as a weakness. This inability to come to terms with your (or anyone else's!) emotions does create obstacles for you in your personal relationships. New Aquarian, you cannot forever hide behind a cause or a campaign. There comes a time for standing naked without the walls of principle surrounding you.

The Water Carrier resembles two ripples of water. They could also be seen as two conducting rays of light emanating from you, a beacon of righteousness. Water symbolizes intuition and of course, New Aquarian, you are an Air Sign. Water and Air represent the two common elements which link all humanity together. These elements – a blending together of intuition/creativity with reason/intelligence – symbolize the achievement of mental enlightenment. But wait, New Aquarian. Loosen up and take a look at reality. Maybe then your ideas will not appear so 'far out' and people will be more willing to listen to you.

It is strange how on the one hand you are attracted to the unusual and bizarre, while on the other you possess a wonderful gift for logic. You can discuss things reasonably and rationally. You have all the answers and a talent for analysis of the human condition. You see other people as mechanisms, intelligent machines with nothing more than cogs and flywheels inside. Your knowledge is grounded in fact, but really, New Aquarian, is this the way to view others, those whom you are fighting for and wish to help? You ought to take a more realistic approach to other people: they are mind, body and spirit. You take on board the first two qualities, but you often forget the third.

You rarely 'feel' things in the sense of having a gut reaction to something, and you don't really know what it is to follow your instincts. You are a complex Star Sign, now positioned thirteenth on the Zodiac, and of course you have feelings – but you don't know how to deal with them. You can become embarrassed and feel awkward in certain social situations. Everything has to have a reason. You are capable of sacrificing your life for a cause and for those you love, but you find it very difficult to say the words or express the emotion of love. When was the last time you bought your partner a gift, or showered praise on him or her? You can't remember, can you? No, because it was so long ago. If you were asked, 'How do you feel about so and so?', you would answer by presenting the logical case for and against the subject, stating your position with some passion but arriving at your conclusion purely through logical thought. You would never say, as other Star Signs do, 'I feel it is wrong (or right), but I don't know why. It just "feels" that way.'

What can be done to reconcile the abstract love you have for humanity with the feelings you have for those close to you? Generosity to yourself and those close to you is part of your 'ideal' love. But, New Aquarian, you miss the point. Love isn't about ideals. You find it difficult to relate to others because you possess too much sense of the ideal and too little of the 'personal'. Your ideals zoom right off the planet because you lack this sense of 'self'. New Aquarian, your humanitarian achievements are great and you have so much to be proud of, but remember this: you are also human. Try not to neglect this aspect of your being. Water Carrier, you must at some stage carry your own water and not that of others. Your need to be liked and admired by others must, occasionally, be resisted. No, I am not saying that you promote a cause just to be admired. You really do believe in the causes you support. You have a Star Sign of integrity and you are a compassionate person. But in the end everyone values you for yourself, not for the activities and charities you so energetically promote.

Actress Elizabeth Taylor is a new Aquarian and so typical of this Sign. One of the freest spirits in the Hollywood movie industry, Liz is generous beyond belief and very talented. Throughout her professional life she has involved herself with numerous good causes, crusading on behalf of others. Liz has raised millions of dollars for charity. One is not surprised by the fact that Liz has had several partners, all of whom have loved her deeply and been made happy by her. She is one of the most prestigious people in the whole of Hollywood.

One look at Jon Bon Jovi and immediately it hits you: he's a New Aquarian and no mistake! Leader of one of the most successful American rock bands of all time, he is inventive, imaginative and a very nice person to have as a friend. His reforming nature drives him to fight crusades against injustice wherever he finds it. He is adored the world over for his youthful yet rugged looks, his unmistakable voice and the way his band is so 'together'.

Love and Relationships

You live in a world of ideas and are a bit scared of your emotions. When you are in love you are adorably naïve and you display behaviour patterns which are quite opposite to those you normally exhibit. Your many talents are not best served in the realms of love and romance. You want to be faithful to your lover, but you have an independent nature and a dispassionate, detached manner which can lead to many broken hearts.

You are a truth addict, but when your partner asks you how you think he or she looks you should *not* say: 'Well, pretty terrible, actually' (well, only as a joke – never if you really mean it!) You must learn to be economical with the truth when it comes to affairs of the heart. Your partner is asking for a compliment, not the absolute truth. The next time you are asked this question, just say, 'You look absolutely ravishing and I could eat you up', then give your partner a big sloppy kiss! That is how it is done if you wish to keep your lover happy, and you do.

You are more than capable of keeping promises because you are a lover of honesty and a natural truth-teller. It's beyond your comprehension that someone could actually make a promise without any intention of keeping it. If you promise to be faithful to your lover, you mean it. However this is not at all difficult for you, so we needn't admire your morals too much. Because you are oblivious to the world of romance and in many affectionate situations you feel awkward and unsure of yourself, you find it much less bothersome to remain loyal to your lover than to have a string of affairs. You are passionate about your latest cause, but you are not so passionate with your lover. Friendship often means so much more to you than love, partly because you find love such a difficult subject to understand. Friendship is easier for you, and you do make a marvellous friend, loyal and capable of self-sacrifice. You are a good listener and no friend could be more tolerant than you. You like a relationship to be without the emotional baggage and clutter of a love affair.

You are probably the least possessive of all the Star Signs and believe in giving your partner a lot of freedom. If your partner is looking for a romantic, intimate affair, he or she will be disappointed. If your partner wishes to get involved in a heated discussion on Marxism or Friedman's economic philosophy, you will happily comply. For heaven's sake, New Aquarian, try to get your passion fired up in the direction of your partner. Your lover would rather hear sweet nothings and be kissed and cuddled than listen to the Gettysburg address, so make the effort.

Many lovers say that their partner is also their friend, and in the case of the New Aquarius person you are the best friend any lover could have. You are genuinely interested in your partner so long as there is no heavy emotional involvement.

Many long-standing relationships involving New Aquarians are successful if their partners have some kind of hobby. The other New Star Signs share little of your enthusiasm for a partner's interests, so this is a point worth mentioning. Your interest in your partner's pastimes is a real plus for the New Aquarian. You can often be seen with your partner at craft fairs, exhibition centres or galleries. Your partner feels really privileged and humbled that you share his or her interest. You are not deliberately feeding your partner's ego, but that's the result and it works to your advantage. Your partner feels really good about you and, at the same time, slightly guilty because he or she does not share your interests. Heaven forbid! You don't want your partner involved in your latest cause, he or she would drive you crazy and you value your independence too much. You satisfy your partner and are thus free to pursue your own causes.

Your ideal partner would be a New Virgoan or New Capricornian, or perhaps a New Ophiuchan or New Cancerian. These Star Signs have the qualities to complement your personality and you will get on really well with them. The New Ophiuchan has empathic powers, and if you are afraid to show your emotions the Serpent Bearer will feel and display them for you.

Career

You are intelligent and full of reforming ideas. You are broad-minded and have the ability to synthesize. All these qualities should influence the direction your career will take. Forget chiropody, sailing or being a psychic medium; these are not the careers for you, as your old Star Sign's advice predicted. Not at all! You are clinical as well as possessing reforming abilities and you want neither a boring job nor one which demands too much of you emotionally.

You are a dealer in truth. You love to record the truth and observe the truth – and as a scientist, photographer, writer or broadcaster your natural commitment to veracity could be utilized. If a media organization wished to hire a factual news reporter and the job description stated, 'The applicant must be able to report the truth accurately', then the position would be filled by you – the other applicants just wouldn't stand a chance. This is the type of person you are: a truth-seeker. If you had any psychic leanings you would make a good astro-psychologist, but as you haven't – too bad.

Although you care about life's marginals, you

would not be suited to a career in the 'caring and health' professions. You are far too detached. As a campaigner on behalf of the underdog, well, your only paid role would be as a high-profile leader, perhaps of a national charity supporting your favourite cause.

You are hopeless with money and let it slip through your fingers. You are swayed towards the bohemian lifestyle and do consider money purely as a means to an end. It's there for spending, not for saving or investing. Take my advice: let your partner look after the money. I had a New Aquarian friend and every month he took his pay cheque and spent the lot, not maliciously, on whatever took his fancy. At the end of each month he had nothing left to pay the bills and was always in arrears and, consequently, in trouble with his bank manager. I advised him to let his partner look after the finances.

Having said this, your talents will always keep you in full employment and you can look forward to a happy and exciting career in the field of your choice.

Health

Poor old ankles and knees. You are dashing around promoting this cause and that cause when suddenly you twist your ankle (again!) You really must learn to slow down and stop rushing around from place to place. The crusade will still be there tomorrow, with or without you. Your knees are vulnerable and, sometimes, your circulatory system can give you cause for concern.

Surprisingly, the best cure for aching knees and

poor circulation is exercise. No, not running the mile in under three minutes, but a more gentle and less strenuous exercise: walking, preferably in the countryside where you can also inhale lots of fresh air. And my word, do your lungs need fresh air! All that campaigning in smoke-filled village halls and public houses means your lungs are positively craving fresh air. You must learn to take better care of yourself if you are to be of use to anyone. Remember the first rule of the paramedic: be safe. When paramedics are called to an emergency, they first check the safety of the accident vicinity. If it is not safe, the medics do not go in there. They protect their own safety first. (What use are they to anyone if they are injured themselves, or dead?) You must do the same. If you are poorly through your own self-neglect, how will you fight the good fight? Get a few early nights.

Because of your 'far-out' causes your diet may also be 'far out'. It is good to eat an alternative diet, but not *too* alternative. What is wrong with simple, ordinary meals now and again, so long as they are wholesome? Cut out all that spicy, exotic food for a while, it will do you good. You are a warm-blooded creature and are carrying that which sustains all life: water. Try drinking a little yourself.

On the whole you enjoy good health, with only minor ailments (mostly during the winter months).

Future

The Water Carrier likes to live in a place where water flows abundantly. Your alternative and crusading lifestyle is a constant joy to you. Yes, you would really like to practise a true bohemian lifestyle, but your logical mind dictates that it is impossible. Your ideas are way in advance of their time and you know that what you are doing now is planting the seeds of hope. It will be the generations of the future who will benefit from your deeds.

New Aquarian, your relationship with your partner will flourish and grow. The longer you are together the more tolerant and understanding of each other you will become. You are so lucky, New Aquarian, and everything is going just as you planned. Your New Star Sign reflects the truth about you, in a way that your traditional Sign never could. You are a crusader for the truth and you have right on your side. Your life is rich and fulfilled, and the clear, life-giving water which is surging all around you will fill your life with happiness.

Appendix

*Famous People Born under the
13 New Star Signs*

New Pisces: 12 March to 18 April

Marlon Brando
Michael Caine
Glenn Close
Aretha Franklin
Holly Hunter

Spike Lee
Liza Minelli
Eddie Murphy
Kurt Russell
William Shatner

New Aries: 19 April to 13 May

André Agassi
Daniel Day-Lewis
Emilio Estevez
Ella Fitzgerald
Bianca Jagger

Dudley Moore
Michelle Pfeiffer
Paloma Picasso
Brooke Shields
Barbra Streisand

New Taurus: 14 May to 20 June

Cher
Eric Clapton
Bob Dylan
Clint Eastwood
Michael J. Fox

Janet Jackson
Grace Jones
Paul McCartney
Priscilla Presley
Gabriela Sabatini

New Gemini: 21 June to 19 July

Dan Aykroyd	Nick Faldo
Kathy Bates	Harrison Ford
Mel Brooks	Tom Hanks
Bill Cosby	Anjelica Huston
Tom Cruise	Kris Kristofferson

New Cancer: 20 July to 19 August

Robert De Niro	Jonathan Miller
Melanie Griffith	Arnold Schwarzenegger
Dustin Hoffman	Patrick Swayze
Whitney Houston	Daley Thompson
Madonna	Andy Warhol

New Leo: 20 August to 15 September

Anne Bancroft	Michael Jackson
Sean Connery	Shelley Long
Richard Gere	Oliver Stone
Barry Gibb	Raquel Welch
Lenny Henry	Barry White

New Virgo: 16 September to 30 October

Julie Andrews	Bill Murray
Hillary Rodham Clinton	Julia Roberts
Michael Douglas	Bruce Springsteen
Bob Geldof	Sting
Kevin Kline	Sigourney Weaver

New Libra: 31 October to 22 November

Boris Becker
Jamie Lee Curtis
Jodie Foster
Whoopi Goldberg
Goldie Hawn

Mariel Hemingway
Dolph Lundgren
Demi Moore
Tatum O'Neal
Meg Ryan

New Scorpio: 23 to 29 November

John Alderton
Ian Botham
Jacques Chirac
Billy Connolly
Ed Harris

Jonathan Kaplan
Imran Khan
Bruce Lee
Tina Turner
Ernie Wise

New Ophiuchus: 30 November to 17 December

Woody Allen
Joan Armatrading
Kim Basinger
Jeff Bridges
Judi Dench

Gary Lineker
John Malkovich
Bette Midler
Richard Pryor
Mel Smith

New Sagittarius: 18 December to 18 January

Kirstie Alley
Nicholas Cage
Kevin Costner
Jane Fonda
Mel Gibson

Diane Keaton
Nigel Kennedy
Annie Lennox
Steven Spielberg
Kiefer Sutherland

New Capricorn: 19 January to 15 February

Buzz Aldrin	Jack Lemmon
Natalie Cole	Paul Newman
Michael Crawford	Dolly Parton
Geena Davis	Tom Selleck
Peter Gabriel	Oprah Winfrey

New Aquarius: 16 February to 11 March

Douglas Adams	Rik Mayall
Matt Dillon	Sidney Poitier
George Harrison	Nina Simone
Jon Bon Jovi	Elizabeth Taylor
Ivan Lendl	Julie Walters

Of further interest...

Chinese Love Signs

*Are you a sensual horse, an amorous goat
or a seductive snake?*

Neil Somerville

In this fascinating new book about the 12 signs
of the Chinese zodiac, best-selling author Neil
Somerville looks at the personalities of each sign,
how they relate to each other – and how they react
when in love.

Chinese Love Signs will guide you towards the sign
which will bring you the most happiness and the
perfect love match. It will also show how you can
make the most of relationships with friends, business
associates and your children. You will discover many
intriguing aspects of your personality and your
strengths and weaknesses will become clear.

This intriguing book makes compelling reading
and contains a wealth of revealing information!

Who am I?

Personality types for self-discovery

Robert Frager

'Who am I?' is the basic question driving interest in personal development and has been asked throughout the ages. There are many different psychological, spiritual and esoteric systems of personality types that can help us find an answer. Here, for the first time, Robert Frager brings together key extracts and commentaries from the world's leading experts in their fields, including Freud, Jung, Liz Greene, Sun Bear, Deepak Chopra, Karen Horney and Ram Dass, to reveal universal patterns of human behaviour.

From ancient systems such as astrology, the Tarot, chakras, medicine wheels and the Enneagram to the latest thinking on leadership styles and body types, these fascinating theories will deepen our understanding of our own personality patterns and those of others.

Step by Step Tarot

Terry Donaldson

Step by Step Tarot is a course aimed at demystifying Tarot reading. It will have an equal appeal for both the beginner and the more experienced student. Whether you feel that you are psychic or have a more down-to-earth interest, this book will give you the training you need to start working with the Tarot. If you have been studying the subject but do not feel confident enough to read for other people, this is an ideal book to help you develop your skills.

The workbook guides you through a practical course that is very easy to use. It gives helpful advice on choosing the right pack and learning the individual meanings of the cards.

Terry Donaldson has over 20 years' experience as a Tarot reader and teacher, having trained over 1,000 people. He is the founder and director of the London Tarot Centre.

I Ching

The shamanic oracle of change

Translated by Martin Palmer, Jay Ramsay, with Zhao Xiaomin

For more than 3,000 years the *I Ching* has been used as a source of guidance, divination and inspiration that directly addresses the heart of the human condition. However, until now the oracle's cryptic symbolism has obscured the dramatic historical event that gave rise to this great work.

The authors of this new, beautifully designed translation have not only returned to the earliest meaning of the Chinese characters but also to the original source of the oracle: to the shaman seated on a cloudy mountain top in Shensi province. Through painstaking research and an astounding feat of detective work, they have uncovered an epic period in Chinese history, a momentous conflict that gave rise to the *I Ching*. Here they tell this long-forgotten story and present the *I Ching* itself, with all its timeless wisdom.

Prophecy and Prediction in the 20th Century

Charles Neilson Gattey

Despite the many theories which attempt to explain it, precognition remains a mystery. *Prophecy and Prediction in the 20th Century* brings us a step closer to understanding the phenomenon.

The cases examined here include:

- the astrologer who predicted Hitler's rise and fall
- the two Dutch psychic crimebusters
- the psychic hypnotist consulted by Stalin

as well as many ordinary men and women who have foreseen future events.

Lucidly written and meticulously researched, this engrossing book is essential reading for the believer, the sceptic and the scholar. Charles Neilson Gattey has assembled the best evidence, both anecdotal and experimental, to provide an objective and comprehensive reference book.

Nostradamus:
Visions of the Future

J. H. Brennan

In this astounding book you will meet a man who
died in 1566, yet somehow:

- foretold the French Revolution of 1789
- foresaw the rise and fall of the British Empire
- traced the fate of popes and kings across four
  centuries and more
- predicted the last two World Wars in gory detail
  after detail
- prophesied the atomic bombing of Hiroshima, the
  first moon landing, the Gulf War...and much more

Nostradamus has also predicted:

- a cure for AIDS
- nuclear explosions over France and in the Aegean
- a massive earthquake that will cause half of Britain
  to sink into the sea
- world-wide famine so extreme that people will be
  forced to eat tree roots
- the arrival of an extra-terrestrial life form in 1999

Nostradamus was right about our past. Dare we
believe that he was right about our future?

Beneath the Wings of Angels

Autobiography of a medium

Billy Roberts with Fiona Roberts

Billy Roberts is a medium who has been to the gates of death many times, returning on each occasion with a message of hope and love. Born with extraordinary psychic gifts, he has survived extreme bad health to become one of the most remarkable and unconventional mediums in Britain.

This book is a down-to-earth and often humorous account of Billy's life. Born into a Liverpool family that was familiar with psychic phenomena, Billy's encounters with the spirit world started at a very early age, guiding him through his years as a rock musician and helping him to emerge from drug addiction. Eventually he accepted the reality of his gifts and became a working medium.

Through his work as teacher, healer and medium, Billy has helped many other people find their own courage and inspiration.

Psychic Counselling

Liz Hodgkinson

Psychic counselling is becoming ever more popular. But what is it and how does it work?

This book demystifies the world of psychic counselling and therapy, and offers an objective and practical guide to all those interested in this kind of help, even the out-and-out sceptic. Many different methods are covered, including dowsing, pyramid healing, aura reading, astrology, Tarot, crystal balls and channelling. The nature of psychic powers is also discussed, together with former and current theories on the paranormal.

At heart, psychic counselling is just one way of helping people to become more positive and to clarify their goals and aims in life. An open-minded view of the subject can prove very rewarding, enabling us to take charge of our lives and gain in confidence. This straightforward and comprehensive overview sheds valuable light on this intriguing world.

The Power of Compassion

The Dalai Lama

Many people have asked the Dalai Lama to address the current difficulties facing humanity. In these talks given in London he speaks about a wide range of issues, including Bosnia, racial hatred, gender and environmental protection.

Modern life is so full of confusion and suffering that people need the courage to face their anger and hatred, in order to transform their lives and relationships.

The Dalai Lama describes in a clear and simple style how to live and die well and how to bring wisdom and compassion into our everyday lives.

CHINESE LOVE SIGNS	1 85538 405 1	£4.99	☐
WHO AM I?	1 85538 425 6	£7.99	☐
STEP BY STEP TAROT	1 85538 431 0	£6.99	☐
I CHING	1 85538 416 7	£12.99	☐
PROPHECY AND PREDICTION IN THE 20TH CENTURY	1 85030 830 5	£7.99	☐
NOSTRADAMUS: VISIONS OF THE FUTURE	1 85538 145 1	£4.99	☐
BENEATH THE WINGS OF ANGELS	1 85538 481 7	£4.99	☐
PSYCHIC COUNSELLING	1 85538 350 0	£ 9.99	☐
THE POWER OF COMPASSION	1 85538 451 5	£6.99	☐

All these books are available from your local bookseller or can be ordered
direct from the publishers.
To order direct just tick the titles you want and fill in the form below:

NAME: _____

ADDRESS: _____

_____

_____ POSTCODE: _____

Send to: Thorsons Mail Order, Dept 3, HarperCollins*Publishers*,
Westerhill Road, Bishopbriggs, Glasgow G64 2QT.
Please enclose a cheque or postal order or your authority to debit your
Visa/Access account—

CREDIT CARD NO: _____

EXPIRY DATE: _____

SIGNATURE: _____

—to the value of the cover price plus:
UK & BFPO: Add £1.00 for the first book and 25p for each additional
book ordered.
Overseas orders including Eire: Please add £2.95 service charge. Books
will be sent by surface mail but quotes for airmail despatches will be
given on request.

**24 HOUR TELEPHONE ORDERING SERVICE FOR ACCESS/VISA
CARDHOLDERS—TEL: 041 772 2281.**